W9-BPJ-596

ATTRACTING
BUTTERFLIES
TO YOUR GARDEN

ATTRACTING
BUTTERFLIES
TO YOUR GARDEN

JOHN & MAUREEN TAMPION

GUILD OF MASTER
CRAFTSMAN PUBLICATIONS

First published 2010 by
Guild of Master Craftsman Publications Ltd
Castle Place, 166 High Street, Lewes,
East Sussex BN7 1XU

This title has been created using material previously published in
How to Attract Butterflies to your Garden (first published 2003)

Text and photographs © John and Maureen Tampion, 2010
Copyright in the Work © GMC Publications Ltd, 2010

ISBN: 978-1-86108-856-7

All rights reserved

The right of John and Maureen Tampion to be identified as the authors of
this work has been asserted in accordance with the Copyright, Designs and
Patents Act 1988, sections 77 and 78.

No part of this publication may be reproduced, stored in a retrieval system or
transmitted in any form or by any means without the prior permission of the
publisher and copyright owner.

Whilst every effort has been made to obtain permission from the copyright
holders for all material used in this book, the publishers will be pleased to
hear from anyone who has not been appropriately acknowledged and to
make the correction in future reprints.

The publishers and authors can accept no legal responsibility for any
consequences arising from the application of information, advice or
instructions given in this publication.

A catalogue record for this book is available from the British Library.

Associate Publisher: Jonathan Bailey
Production Manager: Jim Bulley
Managing Editor: Gerrie Purcell
Senior Project Editor: Virginia Brehaut
Copy Editor: Sarah Doughty
Managing Art Editor: Gilda Pacitti
Design: Studio Ink

Set in Nofret and Helvetica Neue
Colour origination by GMC Reprographics
Printed and bound in China by Hing Yip Printing Co. Ltd

Contents

1 Butterfly basics

2 Gardening styles

3 Plants to attract butterflies

4 Common garden butterflies

5 Breeding butterflies

6 Plants for caterpillars

7 Overwintering butterflies

8 Butterfly photography

Introduction

The value of gardens to butterflies

BUTTERFLIES WILL love to come into your garden if you take the trouble to learn about them and provide them with what they want. The main value of gardens to butterflies is as a place for the adults to find food, and for this even the smallest, maybe as small as a window box or a hanging basket, can be useful.

Your plants must bloom at the time the butterflies are flying, and they must have nectar-producing flowers of the right shape so that the butterflies can actually get to the nectar. Butterflies

▲ **This small tortoiseshell finds the nectar-rich flowers of buddleja an ideal place to feed.**

Did you know?

Like bees, butterflies are insects yet they are not often thought of as being pollinators of flowers and are less efficient than bees in collecting pollen on their legs and bodies. There are, however, some flowers that are meant to be pollinated by butterflies, such as the milkweed (*Asclepias curassavica*).

will fly over your garden fence, see and smell your flowers and use them as a refuelling station on their journey to find a mate or a place to lay their eggs.

Towards the end of the growing season, some butterflies may linger in a favourable garden, to stock up for a long period of winter rest. When fruits have become over-ripe in the autumn some butterflies will come to them, along with wasps and other creatures, to feast upon the rich sugary juice. If you have provided suitable hibernation places, some may even hide away and stay with you all winter, perhaps flitting out from time to time to feed on any flowers you still have, or just to sun themselves.

The value of butterflies to gardens

IF YOU love butterflies you will know that their main value to a garden is emotional. By your own efforts you may have created a garden full of wonderful plants but you know that butterflies will only visit it because they want to. Butterflies are probably the most visually attractive insects that visit gardens and we can appreciate them for that fact alone. Butterflies may also assist in the pollination of any of the flowers that they visit even if they are not the principal pollinators.

▲ **A monarch resting on flowers of milkweed, one of the plants also eaten by its caterpillars.**

Butterflies are also the prey of other creatures. The contribution that they make to the diet of garden birds at caterpillar stage is generally very much less than that of their relatives, the moths, but there are many other creatures that live in gardens that also prey on butterflies.

Different types of garden

NOT ALL gardens are the same and obviously those with large areas of hard landscaping rather than soft plantings will be less attractive to butterflies. Plants without flowers may be helpful as windbreaks in creating the sheltered environment that butterflies need but they will not, by themselves, encourage butterflies to stay in a garden. Flowers are needed for this, and the preference must be for mixed beds with masses of different flowers that provide nectar over the long period that we can expect butterflies to be flying (albeit different generations or species).

Quantity is also required, but of the right type: for example, double flowers, in which extra petals have been bred to make them look more attractive to us, should be avoided. Often, old cultivars are better than the latest fashionable ones. The use of any sort of pesticide, especially organic types which contain bacteria to control caterpillars on vegetables, and which act like a plague to all butterflies, must be avoided, too.

Gardens large and small

A LARGE GARDEN offers more scope for encouraging butterflies, but even the smallest garden can be made attractive. A sunny aspect is vitally important as most butterflies are only active in the sun, and shady parts will be avoided. Rather than siting a patio in the sunniest spot, consider replacing it with some pots for growing flowers. The cottage style of garden, containing flowers derived from or similar to those found wild outside the garden, is better for butterflies than an exotic garden with unusual species and few flowers.

Town and country gardens

IF YOUR garden is in a built–up area you can really only expect to attract a rather limited number of butterfly species (which are of the type described as mobile rather than colony-forming). However, this need not be too much of a handicap because the mobile species are often the ones that we find most attractive.

The country garden might be expected to attract more butterflies than the town garden, but it all depends on what the surrounding countryside is like. If it comprises monocultures of crops, sprayed with all sorts of pesticides, you are likely to see fewer butterflies than you would in an urban garden. If, however, the countryside is the type of environment in which butterflies thrive, you may get species that would never normally visit an urban garden. The important point to remember is that there is potential to attract butterflies to any sort of garden regardless of where it is.

▲ **The painted lady is a very mobile butterfly, here resting on purple loosestrife.**

The species of local butterfly that may visit your garden is mainly influenced by the overall climate of the area. Local weather and landscape will influence how close to your garden the butterflies will come and whether they will stay to feed on the flowers. The possible arrival of migratory species may depend on weather patterns and the direction of the wind. However, nothing is ever certain where butterflies are concerned and this chapter looks at the many complex factors that determine the number of butterflies that visit your garden each year.

Butterfly basics

Basic principles of butterfly gardening

Location and climate

WHERE YOUR garden is located will determine the species of butterflies that you can attract into it; you cannot expect to see species that have never been found in your country, or on your continent. If particular butterflies do not occur naturally in your own country you won't see those species in your garden. There are very few species of butterfly that do occur all over the world, and even those which are seen in different countries on a single continent are likely to have particular subspecies or strains that are prevalent in different places.

There are, however, quite a few species that migrate from one country to another as adults. These are butterflies that may be seasonally common in a country even though they cannot maintain a presence all through the year, and so must be replaced by new migrants each year. Several of the most common garden butterflies in the UK are of this type, such as the painted lady and the red admiral, although with warmer winters the latter species does seem to be successfully hibernating in a few places.

Climate is the major factor in determining the incidence of butterfly species, and can be affected by latitude, altitude and the relative distance from the sea. The general climate for your part of the country is one factor, but there is also the particular microclimate of your garden and areas within it that can vary widely. This not only affects the butterflies but also the types of plant that you can grow to attract them.

Did you know?

Butterflies have a strong visual sense and prefer flowers that are brightly coloured, such as red, blue, yellow and various shades in between. Unlike the flowers that attract moths, butterfly flowers are not always strongly scented. The flowers will generally be open during the daytime, and do not usually close up at night. The size of the individual flowers can vary widely but when the flowers are small they are usually borne in dense masses so that the inflorescence rather than the individual flowers can attract the butterflies.

Soils and shade

EVERY GARDENER knows that the type of soil in a garden will influence the choice of plants that can be grown successfully. Some plants prefer to grow in a light sandy soil that drains quickly but can become dry soon after rain. Others prefer a heavier soil containing some clay, which retains moisture well but can become waterlogged (or too hard if it dries out). The pH value, a measure of acidity or alkalinity, is also important. Some plants need a soil that is fairly acidic, whilst others cope with chalky, alkaline soil. The majority probably prefer to be just to the acid side of neutral.

Finding out what plants grow naturally in your area and then searching for closely related garden plants is always worthwhile. For the butterfly gardener only plants that grow well in full sun or semi–shade are of particular interest because butterflies do not generally visit flowers that grow in full shade.

▲ **A late-season red admiral sunbathing on a conifer hedge.**

Butterflies and plants

A DULT BUTTERFLIES make use of your garden plants in three main ways as described below:

Nectar First is the desire for all species, and both sexes, to visit flowers for their nectar, the food that sustains them during their adult life. Once hatched from the chrysalis and with their wings fully expanded, the adults do not grow in size. They may require other substances for fully effective reproduction. Males, in particular, often visit mud – or even dry soil – to obtain essential minerals, some of which may be passed on to the females during mating. Nectar is low in nitrogenous compounds and some butterflies will therefore visit things such as dead animals, dung and urine, to obtain essential compounds.

Butterflies only have sucking mouthparts, which means that they can only take up liquid food. The tropical and semi–tropical heliconid butterflies are exceptional in that they collect pollen on their proboscis and by exuding liquid from its tip are able to extract a nitrogenous compound, even though they cannot actually eat the pollen. What they get from the pollen has been shown to extend their life span and promote greater egg–laying.

Botanists have divided flowers into seven main types based on the way the parts of the flowers are arranged with regard to the pollinating insects or other creatures that they attract. By and large the types of flower are self–descriptive: dish, bell, brush, flag, gullet, trumpet and tube. Butterfly flowers are generally of the tube or gullet shape, although flag and brush shapes can also be attractive. In the absence of their preferred flowers butterflies will, of course, visit other shapes of flower that are not specialized for them.

The nectar is usually found in rather narrow tubes or spurs, matching the long thin proboscis of butterflies, and therefore protected from other insects with shorter mouthparts. In general, small butterflies will, as expected, have a shorter proboscis and so will visit mainly flowers with short nectar tubes. Butterfly flowers are generally regular in shape and held facing upright. Because botanists classify plants largely on the details of floral structure, butterflies tend to favour certain genera with flowers of a certain type, such as species of *Verbena* and *Buddleja*.

▲ *Lonicera sempervirens* **is called the trumpet vine because of the shape of its flowers, which are not adapted for butterflies.**

▲ **Wisteria is a spring-flowering climbing plant that is often scented, but the shape of the flowers makes it generally unattractive to butterflies.**

▶ **A comma on flowers of *Ageratum*, which have short tubes that allow any size of butterfly to reach the nectar at the bottom.**

▲ *Callistemon salignus* **is a shrub with brush-type flowers, popular with butterflies.**

Egg-laying A second reason why butterflies, or at least the females of the species, seek out certain plants is for laying eggs. Host plants are generally distinct from those used for nectar and may grow in quite different places. Because most of the butterflies that visit a garden are of the mobile type – which do not stay in distinct colonies – they are unlikely to use the garden for egg-laying, unless you have specially planted the required species of wild plant. Although these plants may be attractive when in flower, they will not be hybridized or genetically improved strains that many gardeners prefer and, in fact, some are quite definitely thought of as invasive weeds.

The caterpillars of some butterflies will only eat one species of plant, and even then only one part of one species of plant. These are described as monophagous. Others, such as the painted lady, have been shown to lay eggs on many plant species, and are referred to as polyphagous. This does not mean, however, that a single female adult will switch between plant species.

Later in this book we list extensively breeding plants for specific butterflies, gathered from observations in different places and countries. You will often find, however, that subspecies of the same butterfly use only certain preferred plants.

Pheromones The third reason that some butterflies visit plants – and in this case it is mainly the males – is to take up certain complex chemicals from the plants that can be used as sex pheromones in the search for a mate. This is only necessary for a few species of butterfly, particularly those in the danaid family, which has mainly tropical and sub–tropical species.

Did you know?

The plant a butterfly used as food when it was a caterpillar may strongly determine the type of plants upon which it later lays its eggs. The first few mouthfuls of leaf taken by a caterpillar may also fix what species of plant it will accept as food for the rest of its life.

Matching the seasonal cycles

TO EVERYTHING there is a season and this applies to plants and butterflies as much as it does to mankind. Without the assistance of a calendar, non–human living organisms have to rely on what their senses tell them about the world around them, and this has to relate to what it will be like in the future rather than what it is like now. Fortunately our planet provides this information thanks to its interaction with other bodies in the solar system.

The most consistently reliable feature of all natural signals is the length of daylight or darkness hours throughout the year. Near the equator these will be reasonably equal throughout the year, but as one moves away and towards the poles, so the difference between them in summer and winter becomes greater, with the north and south hemispheres being alternating images of each other. Botanists talk

of long days and short days depending on how many hours of daylight there are in any 24–hour period. Long–day plants flower when the days are getting longer, i.e. summer, and short–day plants flower in autumn or spring. There are many complications to this simple scheme because other factors, such as temperature, may influence the response, and there are also many plants that are not influenced directly by day–length.

Flowering is not the only aspect of plant growth that is affected by day–length: almost all deciduous trees and shrubs sense the shortening days of autumn in their leaves and prepare to shed them long before the weather turns cold. While an adult butterfly may be able to find alternative flowers if its favourite blooms are no longer available, it is obvious that a caterpillar cannot find an alternative leafy food plant if all the leaves have fallen off. So butterflies must also be able to adjust their life cycle to match the seasons and be at an appropriate stage of the life cycle to overwinter in a resting state, known as diapause but more familiarly referred to as hibernation. Depending on the species this overwintering may be as an egg, a caterpillar, a chrysalis or an adult.

In some species the resting state is brought on by the shortening day–length, but in others the actual temperature may be more important. For example, on a warm sunny day in the spring a hibernating adult butterfly may start flying about and then return to hibernation when it gets cold again. While the sort of random temperature fluctuations we tend to get in temperate climates merely slow down or speed up the growth of plants, their effect on butterfly life cycles can be much more serious. In general, the warmer it is above a certain minimum temperature threshold, the faster the speed at which a butterfly passes through the various stages of its life cycle. In a warm year, or in a warm country, there may be two or three generations a year, while in the

▼ **The large white is just one of many butterflies that use shortening hours of daylight as a signal to control their life cycle, allowing them to overwinter as chrysalids.**

Did you know?

As with deciduous plants, the hibernating butterfly eggs and chrysalids generally have a means of measuring low temperatures over the winter so that they do not suddenly start into activity just because it happens to be a sunny day.

cooler parts of the same butterfly's natural range there may be only one generation. There is, of course, always the possibility that a butterfly might reach a vulnerable stage in its life cycle just as winter sets in, instead of being in the correct stage for overwintering. This could completely wipe out the population, and some butterflies have overcome this by genetically determining that there will only be one generation per year, as in the case of the brimstone in the British Isles.

Where do butterflies come from?

▲ *Papilio machaon* is rare in the UK but quite common in Europe, America and elsewhere, but there are many subspecies and races. The UK subspecies has only a very local population, and will not be seen in gardens.

Local populations

SOME BUTTERFLY species prefer to stay in small colonies, and at some distance from other similar colonies, rather than group themselves together into one large population. Such butterflies do not stray far from their home territory, so unless your garden is very close to one of these localized colonies, these species are unlikely to find their way into it. Even if you offer truly floral feasts for them, by providing the exact conditions and biodiversity of plant species, you may not be able to entice them in of their own accord. In general these butterfly species, and others that have very exacting habitat requirements, are likely to be locally common, but rare in the wider picture of, say, national availability.

Long-distance travellers

THE VAST majority of garden butterflies belong to the category of mobile species, of which we can distinguish two main types.

First there are the species that breed in sites that contain all the necessary habitat requirements for successful egg laying, but the adult butterflies are strong fliers and travel long distances to feed and seek mates. Although their flight paths are usually influenced by wind direction, they are essentially random paths, and the butterflies are just as likely to visit a garden as they are any other piece of the countryside.

▲ **The small white is considered a pest species that has been spread by human influence, not by natural long-distance migration.**

At this point there are three big ifs:

• If you have stocked your garden with suitable nectar plants you will reap the benefits because the butterflies will stay around to feed.

• If you have areas with suitable caterpillar food plants in them you can even expect the females to lay some eggs on the plants while they are there.

• If your garden is large enough you may even find that some species set up a territory there and stay for a long time.

Territorial behaviour in butterflies is quite common. Usually it is the males that establish the territories, sometimes around preferred perching sites and sometimes over a defined flight path. They will fly up towards anything that looks like a potential mate, until they get close enough to distinguish potential mates from unsuitable ones, or other butterfly species. In the case of the long–distance travelling butterfly, however, these territories may be a long way away from where the adult actually emerged from its chrysalis – clearly a different situation from that of the colony–forming butterflies.

Migrating butterflies

THE SECOND type of mobile butterfly comprises the species that undertake true migrations year after year, along well–defined flight paths and driven by an innate urge to travel in a particular direction. The classic example of this is the migratory habit of the monarch butterfly in North America. The main requirement here is a long–lived adult butterfly that can overwinter in one place and then move to another along the migration path – in the same way that many species of birds do.

The term migration is, however, often also applied to the situation where freshly emerged adults (which have not overwintered as adults), move in a more or less constant direction to a new area for breeding. These new areas are likely to be ones further north as the weather improves with the changes from winter to spring and summer, the warmer conditions allowing for successful breeding. In the southern hemisphere the directions will, of course, be opposite to those in the northern hemisphere.

Because the period of time during which a fertilized female lays her eggs is often only a matter of a few weeks, this limits the distances that can be travelled and it may fall to the subsequent generation to move further north. In many cases there may be several generations in the southern part of a butterfly's range, and progressively less as the range is traversed until there is only one generation in the furthest northern extent of the species. The cold of winter may then kill off all the individuals in these most northern areas, and the species may only re–establish itself the next year by new arrivals from further south. In some cases the situation is intermediate with some overwintering taking place, but with new arrivals from the south supplementing the numbers each year.

These highly mobile species are often to be seen in gardens, but although some individuals may stay for several days or even more, it is often totally new butterflies that appear from day to day, as they move north, rather than the same individuals. In a few cases there is evidence that a reverse movement towards the south takes place at the end of the season. These will not be the same individuals that flew north at the start of the season. Nor are such movements common, nor are they well documented for most species.

Where there are no natural geographic barriers – such as a mountain range or a wide expanse of sea – to these seasonal extensions of a butterfly range, the timing of the butterflies' arrivals further north or south can be predicted quite well. This may depend on the lengthening of the hours of daylight with or without an

associated increase in temperature. Despite many butterflies being strong fliers, there is usually some relationship between the direction and force of the wind and the direction of flight. In some places the direction of the wind is quite predictable from year to year and season to season. In others, however, wind direction and associated weather conditions are less predictable.

Distinct physical barriers will obviously hinder the movement of the butterflies, and predicting the timing of their annual appearance will be less accurate. When the wind is in the right, direction and of a suitable strength, then the barriers may be overcome. When conditions are not right, there may be extreme fatalities along the way and only a few individuals may cross the barrier successfully. With these uncontrollable variables there may be some years when large numbers are able to reach cooler areas.

Other factors affecting migration

THERE IS, of course, another variable that has not been mentioned, which is the number of butterflies available to start the flight. This will depend on the conditions at either the place where the butterflies breed all year round, or where they can overwinter. Bad weather at the roost of the monarch in Mexico or California, for example, can have a serious effect on the numbers available to move north.

Problems in north Africa over the supply of sufficient food plants for the caterpillars of painted ladies, or the outbreak of a virulent butterfly disease, might be reasons why fewer adults of this species reach the UK in some years than others. This would be due to the situation at the start of the northwards journey, rather than to conditions along the route. Conversely, in some years enormous numbers of painted lady adults can fly to the UK. Although they will breed in the UK there is no stage of the life cycle that can survive the winter in the UK.

◀ **The painted lady is a typical migrating butterfly, and is one of the most widely distributed species globally.**

Why so few butterflies?

How many butterflies are there?

A COMMENT FREQUENTLY heard is that there are fewer butterflies now than there used to be. This might refer to as recently as last year, but it is just as likely connected to the situation remembered when one was much younger.

It is difficult to know exactly how many butterflies there are of a particular species. The number of species recorded in a particular area is usually known, and in most cases records exist going back several years. Many towns or regions have active bands of butterfly watchers who record what they see, and pass the information on to people who keep the records. Distribution maps can then be created to show just where particular species have been seen. If a lot of different people scattered over an area have seen a particular species, we can reasonably expect that the species is quite common in that area.

▲ **Estimating numbers of mobile species of butterfly, like the red admiral, can be difficult.**

Transect survey

One way of getting an idea of numbers of a particular species in a given place, is to carry out a transect survey. Choose a strip of land, just a few metres in width, across the area to be studied, and whilst walking along it count the number of butterflies of each species that you see in the strip. Obviously there will be some degree of error: butterflies may get counted twice, but others may be missed. It gives a rough idea of the numbers, for just a little effort. This is suitable for open areas and with species that are not highly mobile.

This approach to distribution can also be used in the garden, taking this as the area of study. Carry out a regular count in a similar manner each time and during optimum butterfly–spotting weather. Such personal records can be combined with those of other people, who have been using the same recording technique preferably, and together they will build up a significant body of information.

A more precise method, but one that requires much more expenditure of time and a degree of skill not possessed by everybody, is to catch and mark individual butterflies and then let them go again. This is only relevant for colony–forming species because it depends on catching the butterflies a second time, and using a formula to estimate the total number from those that are marked against those that are unmarked. If the species is highly mobile, you might not catch any of them a second time because they have flown out of the area.

Fluctuations in numbers

YOU ARE unlikely to see a particular species every month of the year, and this is due to two factors. First, if there is only one generation per year, as with many species in the colder part of their range, then we would expect to see the adults when they emerge from hibernation – if that is the overwintering stage – in the early spring. If the chrysalis is the overwintering stage, then adults will probably emerge and be on the wing a little later in the spring. If eggs or caterpillars are the overwintering stages, then much of the spring will be taken up with feeding and pupation, and it will be late spring or early summer before the adults are on the wing. If a species is unable to overwinter in a particular region, then the timing of its appearance is due entirely to the timing of its arrival from warmer parts.

If there are two generations per year, then we can expect two peaks of appearances of the adults. With three or more generations per year we can reasonably expect some overlap of them, and adults are likely to be flying throughout most of the seasons, providing there is a sufficiently favourable climate.

▲ With several generations occurring per year we can expect to see the small white at any time during the warmer months.

Second, we must consider the longevity of the adult butterflies. Many species have a life span of just two or three weeks before progressive debilitation, or predation by birds, mammals and reptiles, and even getting trapped in spiders' webs, take their toll of the adult numbers. Unlike other stages of the life cycle, adults are not so likely to fall prey to diseases and parasitoids, but they are susceptible to being preyed upon. In general, we know next to nothing about how many adults are killed in any way, but the number is likely to be very much less than those lost at other stages of the life cycle.

▼ Making a transect butterfly survey across a field can give an estimate of the numbers present.

▼ Butterflies that hibernate as adults, such as this small tortoiseshell, are likely to be on the wing earlier than those that pass the winter as eggs or caterpillars.

▲ **The bright red warning colours on this tropical swallowtail show clearly that it is distasteful to predators.**

Adults have many ways of escaping predation. Warning colouration can indicate that the adults are distasteful due to an accumulation of toxic compounds obtained by the caterpillars from their food plants. This is the case, for example, with the monarch.

Some butterflies, such as the peacock, have eyespots on the wings, which are flashed at potential predators to startle them and so allow the butterflies that slight advantage in time to escape. Some eyespots are found on the hindwings of butterflies near to the tail end. These are thought to cause the predator, probably a bird, to peck at the edge of the wing, well away from the vital head end. A butterfly can lose quite a lot of the area of the hindwings without significantly affecting its ability to fly.

We tend not to appreciate a very tatty butterfly as much as we do a newly emerged and perfect one, yet defects like this may not seriously affect the ability of the butterfly to mate and reproduce. In some species one can often see a very worn individual mating with a newly emerged one.

Another way in which a butterfly can use the patterns on its wings to escape its predators is by way of camouflage, called 'cryptic coloration'. This comes into play when the butterfly is at rest or has perched after a brief chase and has apparently disappeared both from our and any potential predator's view.

Some butterflies live for a very long time, even as much as a year, but they have not generally been active for the whole of that period. The longest–lived are usually those that have only one generation in any 12–month period, but complete their life cycle early in the year. Here, the adults feed heavily during the main part of the year while conditions are favourable, before going into hibernation with no activity, to emerge again early the following year to mate and lay eggs before the end of their life span. Where there is more than one generation per year it is generally the last emerging adults that overwinter. Their life span will usually be less than a year, but they will still last for many months, although most of that time they will be inactive.

Butterfly mimicry

Some species of butterfly that are not distasteful to predators mimic the appearance of other species that are. This is known as 'Batesian Mimicry'. In other cases, several different species that are all distasteful may look very similar to one another to warn off predators. This is called 'Mullerian Mimicry'. Mimicry is mainly seen in tropical and subtropical butterflies rather than those from temperate regions.

▲ **Eyespots and bright colours on the ends of the hindwings distract predators from the vulnerable body region.**

▲ **The underside of many butterflies looks totally different from the bright upperside, as this painted lady shows.**

Factors influencing butterfly numbers

U NLESS THERE are plants of the correct species onto which the females of one generation can lay their eggs, there will not be a subsequent generation. Most of the butterflies that visit our gardens will lay their eggs on plants outside of the garden, so we must always have a strong interest in what is happening to the vegetation in the local area. Supporting local butterfly conservation groups and all manner of other trusts and bodies that are concerned about the environment will help to maintain existing butterfly breeding sites and perhaps help to create new ones. You should, however, look at exactly what each group is doing, to make sure that the correct regimes in favour of butterflies, rather than other species, are being implemented.

It is not always enough just to grow a selection of caterpillar food plants: the exact position of the plants and the microclimate around them may be critical for egg-laying. Individual female adults may pass by certain food plants that are normally appropriate for the species, because they are in the wrong place. Genetic differences in certain strains of the butterfly may cause them to prefer a particular food plant or environment in which to lay their eggs.

Much of the research into butterfly populations, and the associated practical conservation work, has been concerned with colony-forming butterflies, rather than the highly mobile and often migratory species that form the majority of the species that visit our gardens. For these it may be the conditions tens or possibly hundreds of miles away that have the most significant effect on the numbers that are seen in our gardens.

Often some of the best places to see butterflies are the completely unkempt and derelict areas of land where little or no management of the vegetation takes place. The caterpillar food plants of some of our common garden butterflies are actually what we humans call weeds, such as the thistles onto which the painted ladies lay their eggs. These plants may be deliberately destroyed when nature reserves are being established or because some law forces agricultural businesses to control them.

▼ **Major weeds, such as thistles, are preferred by some butterflies, either for the nectar from the flowers, or as food plants for the caterpillars.**

▲ **The large tortoiseshell may be rare in the UK because the adults cannot survive the winters. Also, the loss of one of its major caterpillar food plants, the elm tree, has assisted in reducing numbers.**

Climatic conditions

BUTTERFLIES DO not maintain a constant body temperature at any stage of their life cycle, and the air temperature around them has a marked effect on the rate of egg, caterpillar and pupal development. Biologists recognize three main situations with regard to the influence of temperature upon growth.

Below a certain temperature, called the minimum growth temperature, which varies with each species, no growth takes place and development of the butterfly will be arrested until warmer conditions occur. This happens with some overwintering caterpillars. At the extreme lower end of the temperature range, the exact value of which also varies with the species, death will occur.

Above the minimum growth temperature, the rate of the butterfly's development is more or less doubled by every 18°F (10°C) rise in temperature. The caterpillar may, as a consequence, go through its growth cycle twice as fast. This relationship stops, however, at a given maximum temperature (the level of which is dependent on the species).

Because our meteorologists keep good records of daily temperatures, it should be possible to work out how many generations could be produced in a year. Further, we should be able to detect whether or not a change in temperature due to, say, global warming, results in the butterfly being at a vulnerable stage of its life cycle when winter comes.

Did you know?

Controlled experiments can be carried out in special incubators that enable entomologists to find out how growth rate varies with temperature. From this it is possible to calculate the number of days – at a given temperature – for a butterfly to complete its life cycle.

▲ **Basking in the sun enables a butterfly to warm up for flying.**

Unfortunately, it is not as simple as this. It has been shown that there is a mismatch between laboratory observations and those conducted outside. For example, the caterpillars can adjust their temperature by what they do; many like to bask in the sun, and so raise their body temperature well above that which we might read on a thermometer in the shade at a weather station.

Incidentally, many butterflies are only able to get airborne when their body temperature is at least 20°C. This is not achieved on dull days in most temperate climates, so butterflies are grounded until the sun comes out. Flying about increases the body temperature of butterflies, as does basking in the sun. It is generally thought that the sun's heat is most directly used by the body of the butterfly rather than by the wings absorbing heat and then transferring it to the flight muscles. If the weather is too warm many butterflies close their wings when on the ground, and move to point their edges towards the sun, so reducing the amount of heat absorbed. At the same time this makes them very difficult to spot as there is minimal shadow.

Diseases

IN THEORY, most female butterflies can lay more than a hundred or so eggs. If these all survived to produce adult butterflies it would only take a few generations before we were knee-deep in them. Obviously this does not happen and in general the population size does not get out of hand for long periods. Although there may be large numbers at any one time, something usually occurs to reduce them again. Ecologists call this the population dynamics for the species. With 100 eggs laid in the first generation, there would be 5,000 in the second, based on an equal number of males and females being produced. In the next generation there would be 250,000. Numbers do not increase like this because mortality factors kill most of the offspring.

Ecologists interested in population dynamics try to find out which of the many causes of death, at all the different stages of a butterfly's life cycle, are the main or 'key' factors in determining butterfly numbers. Some factors depend on how many individuals there are, and these are called density–dependent factors, and can cause more deaths in large populations.

There are also regulating factors that tend to keep populations at a steady size. There are so many causes of mortality during all the stages in the life of a butterfly that the result is the death of almost all of the offspring from an original 100 eggs. Provided there is just one female and her mate to lay the same number of eggs to start off the next generation, the population size will be maintained at a constant level.

If population sizes are falling there must be a reason. Food plant availability and climatic conditions have already been mentioned, but death is caused by many factors, and disease is just one of them. Although pathogenic fungi can kill butterflies, viruses and bacteria are the major causes of death. There are many different viruses that attack, particularly the caterpillar stage of the life cycle. Viruses are essentially units of genetic information covered with various protective layers and are not capable of growth outside of living cells because they need the functional components of living cells to produce more

▲ **Butterfly lovers will not use any forms of pesticides or weedkillers on their herbaceous borders.**

viruses. As they do this the cells of the host are damaged and the virus particles build up inside to be released when the cell dies.

The chief visible effect of the virus on a caterpillar is that the subject becomes inactive and liquefies internally. Any liquid leaking out of the body is infectious. Some species of butterfly have caterpillars that crowd together naturally, whilst other crowding may be caused by a shortage of food plants for the numbers of caterpillars present. Both instances will result in a rapid spread of the virus. Because the microscopic virus particles are inert outside of the host body and do not need any nutrients to survive, they remain capable of infecting caterpillars – generally by being ingested when the caterpillars eat leaves that are contaminated – for a very long time.

Bacteria, on the other hand, are living organisms that contain much of the functional components that the caterpillars have. Their action is mostly by competing with healthy living cells of a host caterpillar, and producing a toxic substance that eventually kills them.

The result is very similar to the effect of viruses in that the caterpillars become inactive and the contents of their bodies become liquefied (in this case often with a very unpleasant smell). Any liquid that oozes out will be highly infectious.

Many types of bacteria can be cultured outside of living cells on special microbiological media. Viruses, too, can be cultured, but it is much more complicated with these. Both have been used to attempt to control pest species of butterflies by deliberate release of the disease organisms in huge quantities, sprayed over crops

Did you know?

In the case of viruses and bacterial infections, birds may eat infected caterpillars. This is a common method by which the disease is spread from one place to another.

as biological pest–control agents. Unfortunately, both the viral and bacterial diseases of butterflies are not specific to particular single species of butterfly and so there is the potential to kill non–target butterflies as well as the pest.

Recent advances in genetic engineering have made it possible to incorporate the genes that code for the toxic protein into the plants themselves and so make the plants toxic to any caterpillars that feed upon them. This may make the biological control agent more targeted towards the pests on that particular crop plant, but there is also the risk that it may pass to other related wild plants and make them toxic as well. This would have a consequent effect on butterflies that are not pests.

Further, if the Bt toxin is genetically engineered into crops that are also caterpillar food plants, some populations of attractive non–pest butterfly species could be seriously reduced in numbers.

In addition to the viruses and bacteria that kill caterpillars, there are some micro–organisms that work on the adults in an altogether more subtle and less easily detected way. These may reduce the fertility of the adults, perhaps affecting just one of the sexes, and so reduce the number of fertile eggs available to give rise to the next generation. We know very little about such micro–organisms, other than that they do exist.

▼ **The cocoons of the parasitoid *Apanteles glomeratus* beside a dead large white caterpillar.**

Parasitoids

IN THE past parasitoids were often called parasites, but now a clear distinction is made between the two. Parasitoids always kill the host they are attacking, whilst parasites do not directly kill the host they are living on, although they may weaken it considerably. Parasitoids attack the eggs, the caterpillars especially, and the chrysalids just after they have formed and before the outer skin has hardened. The majority of parasitoids are other insects, mostly minute wasps and flies.

The numerical relationship between parasitoids and butterflies has been studied for a long time and is referred to – in this case not strictly correctly – as predator–prey dynamics. At its simplest level it shows that at first the number of butterflies builds up, perhaps because of very favourable climatic conditions and the presence of plenty of caterpillar food plants. Then the number of parasitoids increases, and since each parasitoid female is generally able to lay eggs in or on a number of, say, caterpillars, the effect of a few parasitoids is multiplied. The number of butterflies then falls. This is followed by a fall in the number of parasitoids. These last effects would not become apparent until the following year if there is only one generation per year, possibly much sooner if there are several generations per year.

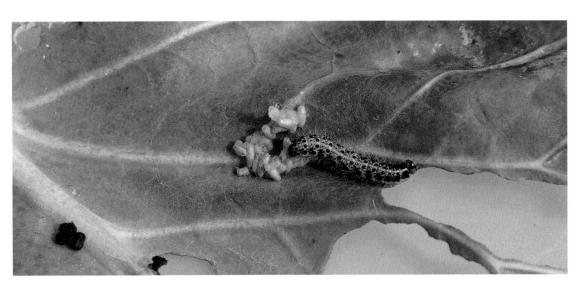

Pest control

One of the bacteria that has been extensively studied for pest control goes by the name of *Bacillus thuringiensis* – or Bt for short. This bacteria produces a toxic protein that is deadly to butterflies, and preparations of this bacteria are used by some organic gardeners, and commercial growers, as a 'safe' pesticide to control caterpillars on their vegetables. It may be safe for the gardener, but not for any of the butterflies that come into contact with it.

The consequence of this natural fluctuation is seen on a graph of numbers present as a wave-like shape with the number of parasitoids just out of phase with the number of butterflies. This is a basic oscillation in numbers that happens, but superimposed on this will be the influence of lots of other factors that can affect the number of butterflies.

Because parasitoids are so effective in reducing butterfly populations, many have been used on pest butterfly species as a form of biological control. There are dangers to this, because the parasitoids are not often restricted to just one species of butterfly, and may prove just as effective against butterflies that are not pests. Many parasitoids are very small and they often have some very odd characteristics. There are some, for example, that lay a single egg into a soft chrysalis as it is just forming, and this egg is then able to give rise to many individuals inside the chrysalis. These escape as fully formed adults through a tiny hole in the apparently normal chrysalis, then they mate immediately and fly off to attack other newly-forming chrysalids. One such species of tiny parasitoid wasp is called *Pteromalus puparum*.

The exclusion of parasitoids from breeding colonies of butterflies is crucial, particularly if one is trying to increase the number of butterflies in a given area.

Predators

THESE ARE creatures that attack their prey and kill it from the outside rather than from the inside (as in the case of parasitoids). Some predators are attractive to have in the garden, chief among them being birds. As part of the natural environment and for the pleasure they give, even the butterfly gardener will generally tolerate birds.

There is concern, however, that the winter feeding of insectivorous or omnivorous birds boosts the bird population to the detriment of the butterfly population. Certainly many birds are significant predators of caterpillars, especially when nesting, and will catch adult butterflies if they can. Mammals and reptiles can also eat caterpillars or chrysalids and may even catch the odd butterfly or two. Spiders are a particular problem for butterflies, both by trapping them in webs and by directly attacking butterflies.

Another type of invertebrate that has an effect upon butterfly numbers is the ant. Some types of ant protect the young stages of particular butterfly species, such as many sorts of blue butterfly (lycaenids), but they may attack the

▼ A crab spider in typical pose, but away from its usual home in a flower, where it can surprise its prey.

⚠ **A tiny black hole in the centre of this pupa is the exit hole for the tiny parasitoid wasp, *Pteromalus puparum*.**

adults if they get the chance. This relationship is a very specialized one that has evolved over a long period of time. Curiously, in some cases it is the butterfly caterpillars that have become the predators of the ants' young stages.

Ants are also a problem for butterflies as they patrol food plants, especially those on which they are looking for honeydew–producing aphids, and they attack and kill anything else they come across. Butterfly eggs may be bitten into and the contents drained out, while caterpillars are killed and the smaller ones generally taken away for food. However, the extent to which ants predate eggs and caterpillars can vary throughout the year; the availability of other foods can influence what they are looking for, and at times they may ignore insect prey.

Social wasps can also take and quickly kill caterpillars, unlike their parasitoid relatives that cause slow, lingering deaths.

Spiders as enemies

Spiders can cause trouble for the butterfly. First, there are those that spin webs in which adult butterflies can get caught. Second, there are crab spiders that hide in flowers and have been known to catch butterflies as they come to feed. Other plant-dwelling spiders are known to attack caterpillars; a very small spider has the capability to kill quite a large caterpillar, certainly one many times its own size.

Pesticides

WHEREVER CROPS are grown and gardens are cultivated there is usually an associated use of pesticides. The major two groups that affect butterflies are herbicides and insecticides. The former can destroy the caterpillar food plants that are essential for completion of the life cycle, and the latter will act directly on the stage of the life cycle that they are used against.

Pesticides come in two basic types – those that act directly upon contact with the insect or plant, and those that are taken up into the plant and are moved around in it, making the whole plant die or become toxic. Many insecticides are used against creatures other than butterfly caterpillars, but will nevertheless kill any stage of the butterfly life cycle that they reach.

Some pesticides are persistent (in that they remain active for a long time after application), but the more recent trend has been to produce short-lived pesticides that degrade either naturally or by biological activity into non-active substances. Although much has been made of the use of natural (or organic) insecticides that are almost always biodegradable, it should be

remembered that they are still toxic to butterflies. Much research has been directed toward pesticides that are selective for particular pests, but in reality any insecticide that will kill a pest species of butterfly will almost certainly also kill non-pest species.

Clearly how, when, where and which pesticides are used will influence the effect that they have upon butterfly numbers, but butterfly gardeners will want to keep away from all such pesticides. And they should try to talk their neighbours out of using them as well!

Human activities

THERE CAN be no doubt that human influence is one of the most significant factors affecting butterfly numbers. This may be to the benefit of certain butterfly species: in many countries, large areas of forest have been cleared and open woodland or grassland has been created – environments and habitats that encourage some species. Unfortunately, the few species that need wooded areas may, as a result, decline.

Certainly the opening up of forestland was good news for butterflies before it became the norm to use intense mechanization, the sweeping use of chemicals and the planting of improved strains of crops. These more recent activities have made the open fields used for crops and animal husbandry less suitable for butterflies, and have brought about a decline in numbers. Organic farming practices may help to reverse this decline of suitable habitat.

Urbanization, particularly the taking of land for housing, industrial development and the associated infrastructure, clearly reduces the amount of space available for butterflies to breed. Planting large tracts of land with alien species of trees, and the improvement of marginal land for agricultural purposes, are also man-made factors influencing butterfly habitats. There are some gains for the butterfly in that the strips of land adjacent to roads and railways are usually left wild, being subject to minimal management of the flora. There is a consequent increase in native plant species, and with them come the establishment of all kinds of animals, including butterflies. The fact that most

Insecticides in plant soil

It is difficult to tell which plants have been treated with systemic insecticides before you buy them from nurseries or garden centres. Vine weevil damage to containerized plants has resulted in commercial plant growers treating the potting soil with strong insecticides. These insecticides are absorbed through the roots and transported throughout the plant. Potting composts treated with these long-lasting insecticides can also be bought, so the butterfly gardener must beware of such hidden dangers.

The definition of a species

There is no single definition of a butterfly species that is accepted by all biologists. Distinctions are often made based on the fine details of the genitalia of butterflies (something that can only be seen under the microscope), whilst some species are variable in appearance and habit. Others are divided up into subspecies, forms and other fine distinctions.

humans are excluded from many of these areas for reasons of safety also allows a semi–natural habitat to develop.

Where houses and other buildings are erected there is generally less chance for butterfly habitation. The tidier the urban area, the worse it will be. Tarmac, concrete and hard landscaping will not encourage butterflies.

Close management of parks, verges and gardens – with grass cut at the wrong times, cut too short, or with pesticides used – can all result in the death of the younger stages in a butterfly's life cycle. Those who are obsessive about creating the most beautiful garden, street or town can, in their search for what some may consider perfection, be harming local butterflies. However, just letting Nature take its course can also result in a poor habitat, as those who maintain butterfly reserves will tell you.

The key is to allow some places to become untidy, but not necessarily overgrown. Derelict, or as they are often referred to, 'brown–field' sites, can often be ideal places for butterflies to breed. We have found, for example, that a small strip of waste ground alongside a road, that had been left derelict, had dozens of butterflies of various species living and breeding on it. Meanwhile, the nearby nature reserve that was being conserved for the benefit of birds had hardly any butterflies!

Finally, a controversial aspect of human activity that creates ill–feeling between the butterfly–loving camps, is the question of the killing and collecting of adult butterflies. In the past, the worldwide collecting of butterflies for scientific purposes was used to find out which species exist, and where they lived. What constitutes a species of butterfly is now generally agreed, but there are still many areas of uncertainty.

Anyone using a field guide should be aware that the names in it are not necessarily the end of the story. It is often not understood that the scientific (Latin) names given to butterfly species are not based upon a written description, but upon a 'type' preserved butterfly specimen lodged in a recognized museum somewhere in the world. The written description comes from that specimen. Museums are the best place for dead, preserved butterflies. There they can be looked after by professionally trained staff, and are usually available to serious students of butterflies. The butterfly gardener, however, should concentrate on creating a haven for living butterflies, and if a visual record of the species present is required, this should be a photographic one.

▼ **Tidy park bedding, with regimented rows of flowers, and lawns, may not leave much useful room for butterflies.**

If you want to encourage butterflies to your garden, you need to create an area that is attractive to them. Since the plants that attract butterflies are mainly sun-loving, flowerbeds should be in the best spots in the garden to attract them. The location of your butterfly garden is crucial. This chapter identifies the type of garden you might choose to attract butterfly visitors, from formal gardens, to cottage gardens and miniature gardens to meadows. Whatever type of garden you cultivate, you need to fill it with bright butterfly-friendly flowers and keep them in bloom for as long as possible.

Gardening styles

Intensively cultivated gardens

Formal flower gardens

THERE ARE many different types of formal garden but they all have in common the fact that they have been designed to attract our admiration rather than that of butterflies. Formal gardens have a certain regularity achieved either by the shape and arrangement of the beds themselves, the accompanying hard landscaping or the way the plants have

been used. One form is the traditional flowerbed seen in parks and large public gardens, with clear-cut geometric outlines and a regularity of flower height, perhaps punctuated with a few exotic accent plants. Here ranks of familiar bedding plants, carefully matched for colour, give maximum impact in an overall pattern.

Within the private garden rather similar schemes can be made but they are generally a little less regimented and can be maintained by organic methods rather than the usually more chemically orientated controls that are financially imperative in public schemes.

For the gardener who wishes to encourage butterflies, there is nothing wrong with such formal schemes – as long as the plants chosen are attractive to butterflies, and these plants are in place when the butterflies need them. Since the plants used are almost always sun-loving, the chances are that the beds will be in the best spots in the garden to attract butterflies. Continuity from year to year will depend very much on the gardener because mostly frost-tender plants are grown for a summer display, and for the rest of the year the beds are left fallow.

Old-style knot gardens, with their clipped hedges of box, will not prove very attractive to butterflies unless the planting in the enclosed beds has been carefully chosen and the areas are sufficiently large to overcome the off-putting influence of the green boundaries. Herb gardens are also not to be recommended unless the herbs are allowed to flower extensively rather than being cut. Where short hedges are required there is much to recommend the use of lavender or the dwarf hebes that can be allowed to flower. It might be expected that formal flowerbeds

◀ **Formal flowerbeds can be stunning, but make sure you choose flowers that butterflies like.**

▲ Blue and pink-flowering *Ageratum* is liked by butterflies and it can be used as a bedding plant.

containing plants from a single botanical family would be good for butterflies. This is not how it generally turns out, however. The tendency is for us to grow only a small number of plants of each species, and different species within the same plant family may flower at quite different times, and have quite different growth habits. By examining the fine details of the sexual parts of the flowers, botanists can see the relationships between different species in a single plant family. It is most unlikely, however, that butterflies will be able to make the same distinctions, unless the family has a remarkable uniformity of floral appearance, which is relatively unusual.

Water gardens or aquatic features are a popular choice for garden designers, but in general they are not desirable to butterflies. True, some species of butterfly have a distinct attraction to damp mud or stones, but this tends to be a feature of tropical species rather than those found in temperate climates. Some marginal plants may have flowers that can satisfy the needs of butterflies, but this is unlikely to be their main purpose because other types of pollinating insect predominate in the places where they grow.

Informal and cottage gardens

THE MIXED arrangement of perennials, annuals and biennials that characterizes informal and cottage gardens provides a continuity of flowering throughout the year. This complements the seasonal variations in the times when butterflies are flying. The traditional plant species and cultivars used in these types of gardens are much less likely to have been subjected to the undesirable influence of plant breeders attempting to produce something better or different for the human palate, without a thought for either butterflies or other pollinating insects.

Although half–hardy flowers can be used in a cottage garden they must be considered an extra rather than a mainstay of such plantings. The regimented rows and flower heights of formal flowerbeds can be forgotten in the cottage garden, and colours can be selected to please the eye of both butterflies and gardeners.

By growing a mixture of different plant species you will encourage natural pest and disease biological control agents. Although some of these may attack the young stages of butterflies, they will not be a serious threat – apart from spiders – to the flying adults. What these agents will do, however, is to reduce the incidence of plant pests, which need to be controlled with a pesticide. Remember that organic (natural) pesticides can be just as lethal to butterflies as the chemical ones that have been prepared in laboratories.

▼ The lily pond in this garden is beautiful, but the water itself is of little use to butterflies.

▲ **Honesty is an old garden favourite, and also a food plant for caterpillars of the orange tip butterfly.**

Patio and container gardening

A GARDEN IN miniature cannot be expected to attract as many butterflies as a full–sized one but it can still be useful if that is all there is room for. Whatever the type, be it tub, trough, pot or hanging basket, the objective is the same – to fill it with bright butterfly flowers and to keep them in bloom for as long as possible. This requires attention to the three main needs: watering, feeding and deadheading, on a regular basis. The containers must, of course, be placed in a sheltered, sunny position and for best effect they should be bunched together rather than spread out thinly.

Design principles and cultivation strategies

The location of your butterfly garden is very important. The eagerly sought–after south–facing garden in the northern hemisphere (or a north–facing one if you live in the southern hemisphere) sounds ideal. However, this can mean that the best part of the garden for a butterfly bed is right next to the house, where most people want to put their patio.

Regardless of the shape of your garden, make sure that you know where the sun is coming from at around midday. Draw a plan of the garden to scale. Find out what is in your neighbour's garden; perhaps they are growing something that will block out the sun – either now or after a year or two's growth. Are they planning to extend the house in any way, which could create shadow on your property?

Calculating the angle and direction of the sun, to determine which parts of the garden will stay sunniest throughout the year, can be difficult. So, if you can possibly delay the installation of your butterfly garden until you have seen a whole year pass and, more importantly, make a paper plan, you will be well–placed to identify the best spots for a butterfly bed. Knowing the prevailing wind direction and planting appropriate windbreaks are also important because rapidly moving air also means rapidly moving butterflies – you, and they, are looking for the garden 'suntraps'.

▲ **A mixed flower border is a sure attraction to butterflies.**

▲ **If suitably planted, wall baskets can add a touch of colour and provide butterflies with a feeding site.**

▲ **A round butterfly bed, with scabious, red valerian and other butterfly-attracting plants, looks very good, but the shady side will be less useful.**

The main orientation of a butterfly bed should be at right angles to the sun so that the long axis points east to west. Unless the planting is to consist entirely of plants that are the same height, any bed will have a sunny and a shady side. Since the latter will not be particularly attractive to butterflies, it is best to have rather longer than square beds, and oval or crescent shapes rather than round beds.

The butterfly bed should be as big as possible, rather than a lot of little beds separated by grass or paving. As a general rule paths should be of gravel or slabs since closely mown grass is not attractive to butterflies but warm gravel or slabs may encourage them to rest and sun themselves. A less maintained lawn comprising mixed grass species and a somewhat weedy appearance is, of course, a different matter and much more appealing to butterflies.

One point that tends to be forgotten is the direction from which the butterflies arrive. If possible, your butterfly bed should be right in front of them when they enter the garden. It should not be situated to one side, in case your visitors fly past it and into the next garden before they even notice it. A little observation and a flexible interpretation of the principle and rules may help at the planning stage. Whenever you plant flowers that attract butterflies remember to be bold, and have a good-sized patch of each colour and plant. Because butterflies have rather poor eyesight make sure there are large splashes of colour. Experiments have shown that an irregularly outlined patch of colour is more attractive than the same area within a shorter, regular outline.

What plants to choose

Choosing the types of plants that encourage butterflies to your garden will be a question of trying to match their flowering times with the arrival times of the butterflies. Since this cannot always be forecast accurately, it is best to plant flowers that have a long season rather than ones that bloom all together for only a short period of time.

Butterfly meadows

The large and the small

A MEADOW IS properly defined as an area of grassland in which a great variety of species of other plants also grow. In most areas of the UK, but not necessarily in all parts of the world, the natural grassland environments have been either maintained by humans or 'interfered with' by domesticated animals. Without this 'interference' the grassland would readily revert, first to scrub, and then to woodland (in fact, wide grassy rides and firebreaks in woodlands and forests are also excellent for butterflies). At the same time, the great biodiversity of species of plants and animals that we associate with grassland would disappear, to be replaced by woodland species. Because there are relatively few species of temperate butterflies that live in a closed woodland ecosystem it is important that meadows are maintained.

▲ A well-maintained coppice woodland is ideal for butterflies with its mosaic of open ground and immature coppice stools.

Different grasslands can be identified by the measure of acidity or alkalinity in the soil. While some species of butterfly can be found in different types of meadow, others may be restricted to only one of them because the food plants for their caterpillars are only found in that type.

The amount of water available in the soil is another aspect of meadowland that has some influence upon the species present. Depending on the rainfall, the topography and the influence of the type of soil upon drainage means there are damp, ordinary and dry meadows.

Unless you have meadows of the right type near you, you cannot expect to attract into your garden the colony–forming species of butterfly that breed in them. Hence there is a real need to support local individuals and groups who are helping to maintain nearby meadows and, if you have the space, to start establishing your own butterfly meadow. Most people cannot expect to have huge meadows of their own. It should, however, be possible to make a useful butterfly meadow in quite a small area, as the butterflies do not generally spread out over the whole of a large meadow but, instead, breed in quite small colonial areas within it. While there is no upper limit to the size of a butterfly meadow, it has been suggested that a tiny plot could provide a useful area of meadow if carefully located and properly maintained. It would certainly be of sufficient size to support not only quite a wide range of plant species but also a number of butterfly caterpillars, if egg-laying can be encouraged.

Natural and enhanced meadows

THERE IS no such thing as a 'natural' meadow, so what we are really talking about is a meadow comprising plant species that have arrived by natural means rather than by human intervention. Almost all soils contain a reservoir of dormant seeds that can be stimulated to grow if the soil is disturbed.

The species growing in a grassy field will depend on the previous human interference. From the point of view of butterflies the best start is with a hay or flower meadow that has not been 'improved' by the introduction of fast-growing and vigorous commercial grasses. It is generally accepted, for example, that ryegrass (*Lolium*

The pH value of soil

It is generally known that pH 7.0 is neutral, with values below this indicating an acid soil and those above indicating an alkaline soil. For every step on the scale of a whole number, there is a tenfold change in acidity or alkalinity. Therefore, pH 5.0 is 10 times more acid than pH 6.0 and so on.

Most species of plants can tolerate soils in the region between about pH 5.5 and pH 7.0, and the tendency is to call such soils 'neutral' although this is obviously not strictly true. Below pH 5.5 the soils and the resulting more specialized vegetation that grows on them produce acid grassland, while above pH 7.0 we are entering the region of calcareous (chalk or limestone) grassland, which again has its own specialized flora and fauna.

perenne) and all its many varieties are unsuitable as food plants for butterfly caterpillars, so a field that has been ploughed up and planted with fast-growing strains of this species is not a good starting point for a butterfly meadow.

Another undesirable feature relates to the use of chemicals in the meadow. If the ground has been subjected to the application of

▲ **Buttercup meadows like these are typical of damp grassland in the UK.**

▲ **A mini-meadow can be established in a small area of a more formal garden.**

▲ **A simulated USA prairie meadow in a UK environment.**

fertilizers, either chemical or organic, plant biodiversity will almost certainly be reduced. Of course, the use of pesticides and selective weedkillers in a prospective butterfly meadow is also undesirable.

The third factor, which then determines the character of the field, is the regime of harvesting that has been used. In essence, two systems can be usefully employed. One is to cut early in the summer, producing a spring meadow that has conditions preferred by some species of butterfly, and the other is to cut late in the year, producing a summer meadow with much taller vegetation and the majority of the grasses at the seeding stage.

Ideally, the butterfly enthusiast seeks to emulate the traditional hay meadow that has been subjected to the same growth regime for decades, and so will have built up a particular biodiversity of both vegetation and insect life. Often a meadow does not contain the range of plant species that one would like to see, and in such cases the meadow can be 'enhanced' by us introducing the missing species. One should start by introducing strains of the missing species that occur locally. If these are not available, then opt for seeds or plants from similar habitats from further afield.

There is much discussion over the use of seeds of plants that have come from another country. Gardeners commonly accept that there are many different cultivars of garden plants, but when it comes to native or wild plants they tend to think that only a single, uniform species exists. This is not true. Plants from a single species from one country are likely to differ in a significant way from those that occur in another.

Some gardeners look upon their meadow as an extension of their cultivated garden. So, there may be little problem for them in planting 'alien' strains; some will even choose to grow exotic species that do not naturally occur in their own country. Such meadows can be visually attractive to their owners but may also bring angry cries from naturalist neighbours and others. Even if there is no law against it, there are many who consider that ownership of land does not imply the right to plant what you like on it, especially if genetic interchange can occur with neighbouring plants outside.

Design principles and cultivation strategies

As WE have seen, the ideal butterfly meadow will be one that faces towards the sun. This way it receives the maximum amount of sunlight. The ideal meadow will also have shelter from prevailing winds so that the microclimate that is produced is one of warmth and relatively still air.

If the aspect of the plot you have is not ideal, some benefit can be obtained by planting new hedges. The effect can be maximized by first developing a ditch and raised bank and then planting along the top of the bank to give a reasonable area of sheltered ground.

It is worth considering bringing some chalky soil into your meadow – if the soil is not already chalky – to form south-facing banks. This will enable you to establish an area of chalk grassland that has its own special flora and fauna amongst the soil type of the rest of the meadow.

If the field has been recently used for agriculture and has been planted with ryegrass and heavily fertilized, it will have a lush growth of grass but few other species. The decision then has to be whether or not to get rid of the existing vegetation by ploughing or the use of a non-persistent total weedkiller, or a combination of the two. This will eradicate the ryegrass but will not reduce the soil fertility, which is essential if a wide range of less vigorous plant species are to become established.

Height of meadow grass

Different species of butterfly have different preferences for the height of grass that they enjoy. Some prefer short grass and others long – while a few are not at all fussy. Short is somewhere over 4in (10cm) – definitely not lower – and neither should it be cut with a cylinder or rotary mower, like a domestic lawn. This would destroy many species of both plants and insects. Short grass could be achieved by a single cut in early spring, or late in the year, towards the end of autumn, which would allow other butterfly species to take full advantage of the meadow.

If you have adopted the clearance strategy you will now be in a position to either cover the bare ground with soil from an unimproved area, or to re-seed the area with a specialist wild flower meadow mix. Care should be taken to ensure that the seed has come from a reputable source and has not been illegally collected from a protected site. If possible the seed should be from a local source and not imported from another country.

During the first few years it may be necessary to cut the meadow several times a year and to make sure that all the cuttings are taken away in order to reduce the soil fertility and prevent overgrowth of the more delicate species. There is no doubt that it will take some years to establish an ideal butterfly meadow to rival the ancient hay meadows that have been under a good regime for decades, or even centuries, but with time and patience it can be done.

◀ **An artificial chalk bank made to encourage plants and butterflies of chalk grassland into a previously unsuitable area.**

If the field you have acquired has been less intensively cultivated, it may be possible to keep the original grass and reduce the fertility by increasing the number of cuts coupled with sowing, or planting, some desirable plant species.

Many conservationists recommend grazing the field with a controlled number of domestic livestock, suggesting that this is the best way to keep a meadow under control. However, this is not always a viable alternative to a cutting regime, and is likely to prove more expensive and difficult for the ordinary person. Whatever method of keeping the vegetation in check, and preventing the ingress of shrubs, trees and noxious species, it is generally considered much better to establish a mosaic of different heights of vegetation, creating differing microhabitats within a field, than having all the vegetation the same height throughout.

The wild garden

A WILD GARDEN is not just a garden that has been left unattended and unloved for years. If you did that it would eventually revert to growing the flora that does, or used to, occur naturally in your area. In many places that might be an impenetrable thicket of trees and other plants with nothing of interest to most butterflies, except at the very tops of the trees.

To attract butterflies you need a managed 'wild' garden in which you assist Nature to provide what butterflies want, and that will not usually be the final (or as some ecologists describe it the 'climax') vegetation of your area. What most books and articles describe as a wild garden is not a wild garden for butterflies.

▼ **A mass of ox-eye daisies in a sensitively maintained mature churchyard that has not been subjected to excessive mowing or herbicide usage.**

They are thinking on a larger environmental scale to attract all manner of animals, birds and invertebrates, many of which will eat the various stages of the life cycle of butterflies. Further, to attract adult butterflies you merely need a profusion of wild flowers, with some blooming at each season of the year. For preference the species you use will be the ones that grow wild in your area.

If you want the butterflies to breed in your garden you will also need some caterpillar food plants. These may not be particularly ornate, or have pretty flowers, but growing them will be your choice, once you know the relevant species and have some idea of suitable places in the garden to plant them.

It is possible to have a combination of formal and wild areas, even in quite a small garden. One of the simplest ways is to let an area of the lawn go wild. Stop fertilizing it, stop using herbicides on it and cut it less hard and less frequently. You will probably not even have to do any new seeding or planting. If you have a little patience some wild plants native to your region will soon establish and spread.

As far as most butterflies are concerned, there is little point in planting wild flowers in odd areas of the garden that are in deep shade and out of sight.

Be bold and embrace Nature by planting good-sized beds of wild flowers where they can be seen. And, of course, plant or sow cultivated native plants or seeds from a reputable supplier, not anything taken straight from the wild. That would not only damage the natural environment, but is often also against the law.

▽ **An area of cultivated lawn that has been allowed to go wild, but is still maintained at a convenient height by mowing.**

Typical butterfly-friendly flowers are red valerian, lantana, buddleja and hemp agrimony. Most are sweetly scented, but some butterflies make little use of scent when choosing which flowers to visit. A butterfly is looking for plentiful nectar, and a corolla (the petal part of the flower) that has a slender tube or spur, without being excessively long. In this chapter, over 40 different families of flowering plants that butterflies will like are listed.

Plants to attract butterflies

choosing plants to attract butterflies

WHAT WE would all like is a definitive list of plants that all types of butterflies will visit. Sadly this isn't really possible. Most lists are made up from butterfly watchers' observations of what has occurred in their own gardens. Therefore plants that are most commonly grown in gardens will tend to be at the top of such lists, while less commonly grown plants, even if they are very good for butterflies, will come low down.

The selection of plants offered in this chapter contains many popular types, but which you grow is largely a matter of personal preference coupled with the location and conditions in your own garden. The distinction between annuals, biennials and perennials is in practice often somewhat blurred. The life span of true annuals must be contained within a single year, of course,

but it is often possible to condense the useful life span of biennials and perennials into one year by cultivation techniques and then discard the plants and replace them with new ones the next year. This avoids the need to overwinter certain plants that are not fully hardy, and prevents others from becoming woody and less floriferous.

Note that the commonly used English name has been used for the alphabetical listing in this chapter. This is because to use the Latin (scientific) name would make it difficult for readers to cross-refer to the many butterfly books that use only the English name. There is a tendency also for plant authorities to change Latin names from time to time, and books quoting them often find themselves out of date fairly quickly. Unfortunately for gardeners, the Latin names of many garden plants often prove to be less stable than the English ones.

Flowering times will differ, depending on where and how your garden is situated. As a guide, the season terms spring, summer, autumn (or fall) and winter have been used, with subdivision into early, mid and late. There are many flowers that butterflies will visit, if the opportunity arises, which we haven't had room to include in this book. Observe which work best in your garden, and for your butterflies, and note them down. But remember that what attracts best in one year may not be as good in the next.

Cultivars within the same plant species can vary greatly, and you need to consider this before you buy your plants. Space does not permit us to give cultivation and propagation details for all the plants listed, but we hope to have provided

◀ **As well as being a cultivated vegetable, the globe artichoke (*Cynara scolymus*) is one of many species in the Asteraceae plant family that are attractive to butterflies.**

▲ **A mass of red valerian, growing along a sunny wall, will be an attractive sight to butterflies.**

sufficient information for you to be able to find this for yourself successfully from alternative sources. The language of flowers is international and most of those mentioned here may be cultivated in any temperate climate. When choosing flower colours remember that some butterflies prefer bright pink and red, whilst others prefer blue, purple and yellow. Flowers of other colours are likely to be less attractive to butterflies.

▼ **The tender Egyptian star cluster (*Pentas lanceolata*), in the Rubinceae family, can be used for summer bedding.**

Directory of plants for butterflies

ABELIA Caprifoliaceae

Abelia schumannii is a deciduous shrub, flowering from summer to early autumn, with tubular lilac–pink flowers. It is rather tender and needs protection in frosty areas but usually re–grows if damaged. Several other shrubby species, some evergreen, are also grown but all like full sun. *Abelia triflora*, another deciduous species, is probably the hardiest. It has scented pinkish flowers.

AGERATUM Asteraceae

Also known as flossflowers, the majority of the cultivated ageratums are cultivars of *Ageratum houstonianum* (sometimes called *A. mexicanum*).

They are mostly used for summer bedding, blooming from early summer to late autumn. Depending on the cultivar the flowers, individually small but borne in dense masses, can be blue, mauve, pink or white. For bedding, cultivars that are 6–12in (15–30cm) in height are generally used. Young plants can be bought in, or seeds sown in a heated propagator in early spring for hardening off and planting out in early summer.

▽ **Pink ageratum is a good bedding plant.**

ALDER BUCKTHORN Rhamnaceae

This is *Rhamnus frangula*, a native shrub of the UK and Europe. The flowers are greenish and borne in bunches from the axils of the leaves on the young shoots mainly in summer. A few cultivars that differ in leaf shape and growth habit are available for the garden, but this is a plant for a mixed hedge, its main merit being as a caterpillar food plant for the brimstone butterfly.

ALLIUM Alliaceae

A very large number of species and cultivars are grown in gardens from the genus *Allium*. Some have edible bulbs – onions – and would not normally be allowed to flower except for seed production, but there are many that are grown entirely as ornamentals. Most bloom in the summer and have massed heads of flowers which stand up from the foliage and come in a variety of colours, depending on the species or cultivar.

▽ **Chives are an ideal dwarf allium species that attract butterflies.**

ALYSSUM Brassicaceae

The commonly grown annual alyssum is now *Lobularia maritima* (it used to be called *Alyssum maritimum*). It is a low-growing bushy plant, only about 3–6in (8–15cm) in height, spreading to about twice that in area.

The normal flowering period is from early summer to autumn, although plants can be bought already flowering for bedding out much earlier in the season. There are many cultivars available and although the most common form has white flowers it is also possible to obtain some in lilac or purple. Grow in full sun, in any well-drained soil. Seeds can be sown in trays at 50–55°F (10–13°C) in early spring, and the young plants should be hardened off for planting out when frosts are over.

The yellow alyssum that flowers from spring to early summer is now called *Aurinia saxatilis* (formerly *Alyssum saxatile*). It is an evergreen, shrubby perennial growing to about 12in (30cm). Seeds can be sown in a cold frame in early spring for planting out in autumn. Cuttings 2–3in (5–7cm) in length can be taken in early summer, rooted in a cold frame in a peat/sand mixture and planted out the following spring.

ANCHUSA Boraginaceae

The blue-flowered *Anchusa azurea* is at its best in late summer. There are several excellent cultivars of this herbaceous perennial, including 'Little John' (dark blue) and 'Opal' (pale blue).

ANEMONE Ranunculaceae

Sometimes called windflowers, there are many hardy species and cultivars in the genus *Anemone*. Those flowering in spring are generally tuberous-rooted, short plants suitable for well-drained soil. The summer and autumn-flowering anemones are fibrous-rooted and ideal for borders. Both types of anemone are available in many different colours.

▲ **The flowers of wild angelica (A. sylvestris).**

ANGELICA Apiaceae

The wild angelica of the UK and Europe is *Angelica sylvestris* and the cultivated one is *Angelica archangelica*. They are short-lived perennials usually growing as biennials, with their umbels of whitish flowers produced in summer.

ANTHEMIS Asteraceae

Anthemis tinctoria, often called ox-eye chamomile, and its various cultivars typically grows to about 30in (75cm) and has summer flowers in varying shades of yellow. Other species are available. The more familiar chamomile, *Chamaemelum nobile* (formerly *A. nobilis*), has daisy-like flowers and can be grown as a scented lawn for areas of light foot traffic. 'Treneague', a non-flowering cultivar, is preferred for this use.

ARALIA Araliaceae

The genus *Aralia* contains hardy herbaceous plants such as *A. cachemirica*, growing to about 6ft (2m) with white summer flowers, as well as shrubs and trees like the Japanese angelica tree (*A. elata*), growing to many feet (metres) in height. The plant once known as *A. japonica* is now *Fatsia japonica*.

ASTILBE/FALSE SPIRAEA/ MEADOWSWEET Saxifragaceae

Astilbe species are summer-flowering perennials in a range of colours from white and pale pink through to red and crimson. It is not to be confused with *Filipendula ulmaria* (Rosaceae), which is also called meadowsweet.

AUBRIETA Brassicaceae

The commonly grown aubrieta (*A. deltoidea*) comes originally from the region stretching from Sicily through to Asia Minor. It is a mat-forming plant about 4in (10cm) high and spreading to as much as 24in (60cm). There are many species and cultivars available, which differ in flower colour and other characteristics, but the most common form has purple flowers. It is a hardy, evergreen perennial but does tend to become untidy with age and is usually then replaced. The plant flowers from spring to early summer

▼ **Aubrieta is an ideal low-growing plant for a dry, sunny spot.**

and likes a well-drained, sunny position, which is why it is often grown on rockeries. Although it can be propagated from seed sown in spring, and with the young plants set in their final spots in autumn, the usual method is by cuttings taken from shoots that have re-grown after the plant has been cut back following flowering.

Take the cuttings in early autumn, about 2in (5cm) in length and preferably with a small portion of the older stem attached (a basal cutting). After rooting they are transferred into pots for growing on and finally planted out the next autumn. When only a few plants are needed or the original ones become overgrown they can be divided in autumn and replanted as required.

BEAUTY BUSH Caprifoliaceae

Kolkwitzia amabilis is a hardy deciduous shrub, which can reach 10ft (3m) or more in height, and bears masses of pinkish flowers during early and mid-summer.

BELLFLOWER Campanulaceae

Many plants in the genus *Campanula* are grown in gardens. As the common name suggests, the flowers are basically bell-shaped although in some the lobes are spread wide when the flowers open. There is a preponderance of blues and some whites among the colours, and the growth habits vary from hardy and tender annuals and biennials to perennials and even sub-shrubs, with some being dwarf plants and others 3ft (1m) or more in height. There is something in this genus to suit almost any garden. The flowers of most species are produced in summer.

◀ ***Campanula cochleariifolia* is an easy-to-grow, spreading perennial with upward-facing flowers.**

▲ **Berberis can attract spring butterflies.**

BERBERIS Berberidaceae

Many species, hybrids and cultivars in the genus *Berberis* are available in cultivation. They are all shrubby in nature and some, such as *B. darwinii* with yellow flowers, are evergreen. Others, such as *B. thunbergii* and its many cultivars, are deciduous. The small flowers are round and cup–shaped, and hang down in large clusters. They are mostly produced in spring. The shrubs usually make dense, spiny growth and some can be used for hedging but require care to avoid injury from the sharp spines when pruning.

BERGENIA Saxifragaceae

Several species of hardy perennials in the genus *Bergenia* are grown in gardens. *B. crassifolia* grows to about 12in (30cm) and has pale pink flowers, while *B. cordifolia* has lilac–rose flowers. Both bloom in late winter and spring. Several other species and cultivars are also cultivated.

BETONY Lamiaceae

The plant we now call *Stachys officinalis* (it used to be called *Betonica officinalis*) is a herbaceous perennial flowering from summer to early autumn. There are several cultivars, and other species, also cultivated.

BIRD CHERRY Rosaceae

This tree, *Prunus padus*, and its improved cultivars, flowers in late spring. It is one of the many types of ornamental cherry available and which may be used by butterflies. Single–flowered forms are the best for butterflies but some cherries are too tall for the small garden and, more importantly, not all will be in flower when butterflies are needing them. The very attractive wild cherry or gean (*Prunus avium*) also has many cultivars available.

▼ **Bergenias have a long flowering period over late winter to spring.**

▲ **Bird's foot trefoil is a tough plant that grows amongst short grass.**

BIRD'S FOOT TREFOIL Papilionaceae

This wild plant of the UK, Europe, Asia and parts of Africa is a herbaceous perennial with a strong rootstock and is a familiar plant of meadows and grassy places.

Its Latin name is *Lotus corniculatus* and its bright yellow flowers, often tinged with red, are freely produced in summer and early autumn.

Cultivated blackberries

There are a number of cultivated forms of the blackberry, which can supply the gardener with fruit as well as the butterflies with flowers and, if properly planted and grown, are much to be preferred. They thrive in any well-drained, moisture-retentive soil, preferably lime-free, and provide flowers during the mid-summer period. There are many cultivars of *R. fruticosus*, some of which are thornless (which has much to recommend it), as well as various hybrids with other species in the genus. To tip layer a blackberry merely peg the shoot tips down in close contact with the soil in early autumn and cut the rooted young plants free the next spring.

BLACKBERRY/BRAMBLE Rosaceae

The wild blackberry, *Rubus fruticosus*, has a modified version of reproduction by seed. This means that the offspring nearly always resemble the parent plant and there is not the usual variation that one expects when plants are grown from seed. Couple this with its ability to readily reproduce itself by tip layering, and the result is many different forms of the common blackberry, some more thorny than others and some with prolific flowering. These are likely to be found in a garden as self–arrivals and it will be a matter of chance whether or not you have a good strain. The plants grow in sun or partial shade and although they may form part of a wild garden they are not normally to be encouraged as they can form dense, impenetrable masses that are good for neither gardener nor butterfly. They can be tolerated in the hedgerow if kept under control.

▼ **One of the many different growth forms of the blackberry; the flowers of all are attractive to butterflies but the plants do need controlling.**

▲ **Sloe flowers are one of the earliest nectar sources for butterflies.**

▲ **Bluebells in a shady spot. In full sun the flowering stems are much shorter.**

BLACK-EYED SUSAN/CONEFLOWER/ GLORIOSA DAISY Asteraceae

Rudbeckia hirta is an annual, flowering from summer into autumn. Other species in the genus are also cultivated.

BLACKTHORN/SLOE Rosaceae

This is one of the earliest–flowering wild shrubs of the UK and Europe and has often been planted in hedges. Its Latin name is *Prunus spinosa*, and for hedge use the single–flowered wild type is to be preferred to the double–flowered cultivars available.

BLUEBELL Hyacinthaceae

The native bluebell or wild hyacinth of the UK and Europe is *Hyacinthoides non-scripta* (formerly in the genus *Endymion*). It is a perennial bulb that flowers from mid–spring to early summer and, although it will grow in open sunny situations, it is thought of mostly as a plant of open woody areas. It is one of the few plants in such areas that early–flying butterflies will visit.

BLUEBERRY/BILBERRY Ericaceae

The edible blueberry is *Vaccinium corymbosum* and its many cultivars. The flowers of this deciduous shrub are white, tinged with pink and produced in long strands in late spring and early summer. *V. myrtillus* is the bilberry or whortleberry, with greenish white flowers produced singly in late spring; it is of less interest to butterflies. Several other species are in cultivation.

BUCKEYE Hippocastanaceae

The red buckeye is a small shrubby tree up to about 10ft (3m) in height, with bright red flowers in erect spires, opening in early summer. Its Latin name is *Aesculus pavia*. It should not be confused with the red horse chestnut (*A.* x *carnea*), which grows to about 20ft (6m) and is a hybrid between the even taller horse chestnut (*A. hippocastanum*) and *A. pavia*.

BUDDLEJA Buddlejaceae

There are some 100 species in the genus *Buddleja* originating from America, Africa and Asia. The most widely cultivated forms in parks and gardens is the Chinese *Buddleja davidii* and its numerous cultivars. It is often referred to as the butterfly bush because it is particularly attractive to many of the mobile species of butterfly during summer and autumn. The best cultivars are likely to be those that have the blue flowers of the wild type, or some shade close to it, rather than the very dark forms.

The flowering period can be adjusted somewhat by the time of pruning because the flowers are produced on current year's growth. Therefore, if pruning is done early the new growth will have reached flowering size earlier in the year, while later pruning will delay flowering. Some gardeners prefer to prune half the bush, and then wait some weeks before pruning the remainder. This results in a longer period of

▼ *Buddleja davidii* **is a tough plant for a sunny position.**

flowering, although the bush may not look as attractive as one that was pruned all at once and then allowed to grow out its arching branches in all directions. Without pruning, the plants can get very tall, and butterfly watching will become difficult. If a compact bush is required, cut back the branches and stems to within 4–8in (10–20cm) of the soil each year – *B. davidii* is tolerant of hard pruning. Cutting off central (or 'terminal') flower spikes when the flowers have faded will encourage lateral shoots to flower as well.

This species, and some others, tend to self–seed naturally all over the garden, but if you want the plants to come true to type then cuttings should be taken in summer. These should be about 4–5in (10–12cm) long, with a heel of older stem at the base, and put into a sand/peat mixture and left in a cold frame to root. They can be planted out the next spring, to grow on before being planted into their final positions the following autumn or even the following spring, depending on conditions. Happily, the buddleja will tolerate almost any soil.

▼ *Buddleja fallowiana* **has some of the sweetest-smelling and most prolific flowers of all the buddlejas.**

Other buddleja species

There are many other buddleja species you can grow. *B. alternifolia* can grow 13–20ft (4–6m) tall, with a similar spread. It flowers in early summer on the previous year's growth and should therefore not be pruned until after flowering. It has a delicate, arching form. Another summer-flowering species, and which carries its blooms on the previous year's growth, is *B. colvillei*. Sadly this species is easily damaged by frost, so in cold regions it is unlikely to reach its optimum height and spread of 20ft (6m), instead making nearer half this. *B. crispa* grows to some 10ft (3m) in height and spread and is also not frost hardy. It flowers on the current year's growth in summer. *B. fallowiana* produces a magnificent crop of flowers which have a very rich, sugary scent. They are produced from summer through to early autumn on the current year's growth. The bush reaches a height of some 10ft (3m) with a spread of about 6ft (2m), but is liable to damage by frost if grown in open situations. *B.* x *weyerana* is a hybrid between *B. davidii* and *B. globosa*. It has clusters of yellow summer flowers borne on the current year's growth.

BUGLE Lamiaceae

Although *Ajuga reptans* often turns up as a member of the community in a lawn that has not been treated with herbicide, there are also many cultivars that can be grown as garden plants. Most do not reach much more than 12in (30cm) in height, but can spread to form clumps of 18in (45cm) or more. The flowers are produced in early summer and are generally a shade of blue. The plants will tolerate most types of soil, but prefer a moist one with some shade. Due to its naturally spreading nature, bugle can be propagated by division at almost any time when weather permits. This species originates in Europe.

A. genevensis, also from Europe, flowers at the same time but prefers a sunny, well-drained position. It can reach a height of 18in (45cm) but spreads only to about 6in (15cm). The flowers can be shades of blue through pink to white.

▼ Bugle (*Ajuga reptans*) growing in very rough grassland.

BUSY LIZZIE/IMPATIENS/ TOUCH-ME-NOT Balsaminaceae

Impatiens walleriana (formerly *I. sultani*), the familiar bedding busy lizzie, comes in a wide range of colours. It is likely to attract butterflies simply because of the vast numbers that are planted in beds each season. However, the length of the tube in the flower means that it will be of most use to long–tongued butterflies, and will be of little use to many of the species that frequent gardens. Other forms of impatiens are also widely grown in gardens, as well as greenhouses and conservatories, but in general cannot be considered butterfly flowers.

BUTTON-BUSH Rubiaceae

Cephalanthus occidentalis is a hardy deciduous shrub that likes a moist but well–drained soil and grows to about 6ft (2m) in height. Masses of white flowers are produced in late summer.

CAMPION Caryophyllaceae

The plants known generally as campions comprise species from several genera and many have their own common names. In the genus *Silene* we have the wild *red campion* (*S. dioica*) and its garden cultivars. In the genus *Lychnis* is *L. chalcedonica* (Maltese cross) and its cultivars; *L. flos-cuculi* (ragged robin) and its cultivars, and *L. coronaria* (rose campion, sometimes named as *Agrostemma coronaria*) and its cultivars. All tend to be short–lived perennials, often grown from seed as biennials, for flowering in summer and early autumn.

CANDYTUFT Brassicaceae

Iberis amara is a fast–growing, bushy annual, which produces white flowers in summer. Other species, some of which are perennial, are also grown.

▲ **One of the perennial candytuft (*Iberis sempervirens*).**

▲ **Caryopteris is a good butterfly shrub, but is rather tender.**

CARYOPTERIS Verbenaceae

Although they are somewhat tender and need a sheltered site, the cultivars of *Caryopteris* x *clandonensis* are well worth growing for their masses of small, tubular flowers in various shades of blue, borne in late summer and early autumn.

CATMINT Lamiaceae

Known everywhere for its ability to attract cats, which often destroy it in their enthusiasm, this is the commonly grown *Nepeta cataria*. The genus itself has some 250 species, many of which have cultivars of garden interest. A native of Europe, the catmint can grow to 3ft (1m) in height and is a hardy herbaceous perennial. The pale purple flowers are borne in summer. It is a close relative of the much smaller ground ivy (*Glechoma hederacea*), which turns up naturally in many untreated lawns and is also attractive to butterflies, despite its diminutive size.

N. x *faassenii* grows to about 24in (60cm) in height and bears lavender-blue flowers in summer. It likes a sunny aspect, but will tolerate some shade for part of the day, and prefers a well-drained soil.

Catmints can be propagated in spring by division from well-established plants, and by cuttings. Seeds will only come true for the original species.

CEANOTHUS Rhamnaceae

The genus *Ceanothus* contains many popular species, hybrids and cultivars. Some are rather tender shrubs but others are quite hardy, and most bear masses of flowers in various shades of blue. *C. thyrsiflorus* is one of the hardiest evergreen species flowering in late spring to early summer. *C.* x *delileanus* [end] 'Gloire de Versailles' is a hardy deciduous cultivar that has very long inflorescences of pale blue flowers from summer to autumn. If space permits there should be one in the butterfly garden, but take the trouble to seek out a cultivar that suits your requirements from the many that are available.

▶ **A ceanothus is always a stunning plant in flower, but choose a cultivar that suits your garden conditions.**

CERATOSTIGMA Plumbaginaceae

Although tender when young these half-hardy shrubs can become hardier with age, particularly if they are allowed to become well established in a sheltered spot. *Ceratostigma willmottianum* is a deciduous shrub reaching about 3ft (1m) in height, bearing small blue flowers in dense masses during mid-summer.

CHRYSANTHEMUM Asteraceae

The majority of cultivated plants that used to be in the genus *Chrysanthemum* have now been placed in other genera (such as *Argyranthemum*, *Leucanthemum* and *Tanacetum*), although they may still be found under their original generic name in many books and catalogues.

▶ **If you grow chrysanthemums, and wish to encourage butterflies with them, make sure they are the single types.**

▲ **Feverfew (*Tanacetum parthenium*) is an easily grown herb that will seed itself around the garden.**

The marguerite (*Argyranthemum frutescens*) is a tender perennial usually grown as an annual summer pot or bedding plant, but can be kept from year to year if a greenhouse is available. The shasta daisy (*Leucanthemum x superbum*) is to be recommended, as is the moon or ox–eye daisy (*Leucanthemum vulgare*). The latter is a conspicuous flower of meadows and there are several cultivars used in gardens. The name 'marguerite' is also sometimes used for this species.

Did you know?

The familiar blooms we all know as florists' chrysanthemums are now back in the genus *Chrysanthemum* after a spell in the genus *Dendranthema*. There are thousands of different cultivars, many with flowers far too double and complex in structure to be of interest to the butterfly.

▲ **Masses of *Clematis montana* grown over a wall can attract butterflies emerging from hibernation.**

CLEMATIS Ranunculaceae

While few of the many species and cultivars of the genus *Clematis* can be considered good butterfly flowers, *C. heracleifolia* is a possibility. It is usually grown as a herbaceous plant bearing clusters of small blue flowers in late summer to early autumn. At one time this was considered to be the correct name for *C. tubulosa*, but that is now considered to be a separate, albeit similar species. The spring–flowering *C. montana* may be useful for butterflies coming out of hibernation.

CLERODENDRUM Verbenaceae

Although most of the members of this genus require greenhouse culture, if you have a sheltered spot outdoors it is worth trying *Clerodendrum bungei*, a deciduous and rather weak–stemmed shrub that produces large heads of rose–pink, scented flowers in late summer to early autumn.

COLTSFOOT Asteraceae

This plant is mostly considered to be a wild and somewhat weedy species of the UK, Europe and elsewhere, but it is attractive enough to be available commercially as a garden plant. *Tussilago farfara* is a herbaceous perennial with yellow spring flowers.

▲ **The early spring flowers of coltsfoot (Tussilago farfara).**

CONEFLOWER Asteraceae

The purple coneflower (*Echinacea purpurea*) is a summer–flowering perennial with purple daisy blooms. It prefers well–drained soil in a sunny position. Rudbeckias are also called coneflowers.

COREOPSIS Asteraceae

A number of species are grown, and they range from annuals to perennials. There are also various cultivars, which differ in flower colour and height. They prefer a well–drained soil in a sunny position. Most bloom from early summer to autumn.

COSMOS Asteraceae

These are annuals that flower in summer and autumn, and which prefer well–drained soil. The most familiar is *Cosmos bipinnatus* and its cultivars, which come in a range of colours. As its name suggests, *C. sulphureus* has yellow flowers while *C. atrosanguineus* has gained favour amongst gardeners because of its dark brown, chocolate–scented flowers, but these are unlikely to be so attractive to butterflies.

▲ **The flowers of the wild crab apple are just as attractive as those of the domestic apple.**

CRAB APPLE Rosaceae

The wild crab apple (*Malus sylvestris*) can still be found in the countryside but in the garden is better replaced with one of the ornamental or edible–fruited apples of which there are innumerable cultivars. The masses of flowers are attractive to all kinds of insects in late spring, and with the advent of dwarf cultivars (grafted forms that would naturally grow to a much larger size) there should be room for at least one in most gardens.

CROCUS Iridaceae

Many crocus species and cultivars are available. These small spring-flowering perennials take up little room and may provide nectar when little else is available.

DAFFODIL Amaryllidaceae

The wild daffodil is *Narcissus pseudonarcissus*, but in the garden there are many other species and hundreds of cultivars to choose from. Typically flowering in spring, daffodils are certainly worth having in the garden. Because there are so many forms available, by choosing various species and cultivars the flowering season can be extended.

DAHLIA Asteraceae

The familiar garden dahlias are of hybrid origin from various species of the genus *Dahlia* and are generally divided into border dahlias, which are propagated from tubers, and the bedding dahlias, which are grown as annuals from seed. There are very many cultivars available and the most interesting for the butterfly gardener, in both categories, are the single–flowered ones. Dahlias flower from the summer to the autumn and like a rich soil which, in the case of the border dahlias, should also be well-drained.

DAISY Asteraceae

The wild, weedy daisy of lawns is *Bellis perennis*, which flowers right through from spring to autumn, but in the garden we can also plant various cultivars derived from it, which have flowers in various shades of pinks and whites, to bright crimson. For preference the less double forms should be grown, but the wild type could also be encouraged in an informal lawn.

DANDELION Asteraceae

The dandelion (*Taraxacum officinale*) is a well-known weed throughout the world in lawns as well as cultivated soil. It is a hardy herbaceous perennial that puts down a thick tap root which makes it difficult to pull up, although it is easily controlled by herbicides. In some countries it is grown for its leaves (for use in salads), its roots (good as a coffee substitute) and its flowers (for making wine). For those wishing to cultivate the

▲ **Dandelions can be weeds, or cultivated plants.**

dandelion, the seeds should be sown in spring, in a sunny position. They will grow in any ordinary garden soil and are visited by many insects, including butterflies.

DAPHNE Thymelaeaceae

Daphne odora is a loose–growing evergreen shrub requiring a sheltered spot, but it repays this attention by producing dense clusters of pale purple flowers from winter into mid–spring. Other species in the genus are also available.

Did you know?

Although dandelions produce a full head of seeds (the dandelion 'clock'), its seeds are essentially a form of vegetative propagation with all the offspring being identical to the parent. This gives rise to many different strains of dandelion, which differ in various characteristics, such as leaf shape.

DAYLILY Hemerocallidaceae

There are very many cultivars available from the genus *Hemerocallis*; the species themselves are rarely grown. These perennials come in a range of colours and flowering seasons from spring to autumn, and prefer a moist soil in full sun.

DELPHINIUM/LARKSPUR Ranunculaceae

In general use, the term larkspur refers to annual species, hybrids and cultivars in the genus *Delphinium*, while the term 'delphinium' is reserved for the perennials. The perennial range, the cultivars of which are mostly derived from *D. elatum* but with complex parentage, is very wide. It is best to avoid the double forms of both larkspur and delphinium.

DICENTRA Papaveraceae

Several species and cultivars in the genus *Dicentra* are grown in gardens. The bleeding heart (*D. spectabilis*) is one of the most commonly grown, flowering in late spring to early summer. *D. formosa* (which is sometimes called *D. eximia* although that is really another separate species) also flowers at this time.

ECHIUM Boraginaceae

Echiums come in a wide range of sizes from the very tall but tender *Echium pininana* from the Canary Islands, to the much shorter viper's bugloss (*E. vulgare*), a species native to the UK and Europe but which is also grown in gardens for its bright blue summer flowers. Other species are also grown, and all are typically biennial. Some can be grown as annuals if seeds are sown early, but a word of warning: *E. pininana* may take three years before it is mature enough to flower.

▶ **The bright yellow flowers of the wild fleabane.**

ERIGERON Asteraceae

There are several cultivated species, although it is mostly improved cultivars that are grown in gardens. They are generally summer–flowering plants available in a wide range of colours and different heights. Although some plants in the genus *Erigeron* are annuals, those that are grown in gardens are mostly perennials, and can be propagated by division or started from seed. These plants are sometimes called 'fleabanes', but this name is better given to species of the genus *Pulicaria*.

ESCALLONIA Escalloniaceae

The escallonias are slightly tender evergreen or deciduous shrubs, and therefore benefit from some protection in cold areas. They do well by the sea. *Escallonia bifida* and *E. rubra* var. *macrantha* are often seen, but the preference generally is for named cultivars. Mostly they flower from summer to autumn. The flowers are available in shades from red through pinks to white.

FLEABANE Asteraceae

Fleabane (*Pulicaria dysenterica*) is a wild plant native to the UK, Europe and parts of Asia. In general it prefers a damp site and is a spreading perennial with bright yellow flowers, growing to about 2ft (60cm). It is grown in gardens for its bright yellow flowers borne in late summer to early autumn.

▲ **Forget-me-nots make a good splash of spring colour.**

FORGET-ME-NOT Boraginaceae

Myosotis alpestris (sometimes called *M. rupicola*), and its cultivars, is probably the best species for gardens as it is a hardy perennial and comes in flower colours from blue through carmine to white, from mid–spring to early summer. *M. sylvatica* is usually grown as a biennial, although it may last a few years. Generally it self–seeds, so needs little attention other than pulling out the old plants after they have shed their seeds. *M. scorpioides* (also known as *M. palustris*) is a marginal or shallow–water aquatic plant that may be useful in very damp spots.

GAILLARDIA Asteraceae

The perennial gaillardia (*G. grandiflora*) and its cultivars flower from early summer to autumn. They prefer a well–drained soil in the sun. There is a wide range of colours available, mainly from red through orange to yellow.

GARLIC MUSTARD Brassicaceae

Alliaria petiolata is also known as hedge garlic, owing to the strong smell of its roots. It is essentially a biennial, although it may persist for longer by forming buds on the roots after the stem has died down. Its preferred location is indicated by some of its names (it is also known as jack–by–the–hedge) and in the garden it

can appear naturally, or be planted, in a sunny position close to walls. Butterflies will visit the flowers produced in spring and early summer. It is of special interest as a food plant for the caterpillars of the orange–tip butterfly, although it is not a spectacular garden flower.

GLOBE THISTLE Asteraceae

This perennial produces globular blue flowerheads in summer, and prefers to be planted in a well–drained soil in the sun. The most commonly grown *Echinops* in gardens is *E. bannaticus* and its cultivars, which now includes plants formerly known as *E. ritro*. Other species are also cultivated.

GOLDENROD Asteraceae

The wild goldenrod of the UK is *Solidago virgaurea*, which grows to about 30in (75cm), although the North American *S. canadensis*, which also grows wild in the UK, is up to 7ft (2.5m) tall; it is an escapee from gardens. There are various hybrids between the species and cultivars; all are perennials, flowering from summer to autumn. There is considerable variation in height between the garden forms and care should be taken to choose a cultivar of the correct height for the site chosen.

GROUND IVY Lamiaceae

This is seen growing wild throughout the UK, Europe and parts of Asia; it can also be a lawn weed where its bright violet flowers add a splash of colour in spring and early summer. The wild species is *Glechoma hederacea* but there are also several improved cultivars for gardens, some with variegated leaves.

HAWKWEEDS Asteraceae

Hawkweeds, with their bright yellow flowers, can come to carpet a lawn as long as it has not been treated with weedkillers. The gardener often finds it difficult deciding exactly which species of *Hieracium* is present, but makes no difference to butterflies who will visit the flowers. Some species are widely available for cultivation and others, such as *H. aurantiacum*, have now been moved to the genus *Pilosella*.

HEATHERS/HEATHS Ericaceae

Species and cultivars of *Calluna* are generally called heathers, whilst those from the genus *Erica* are the heaths, but this distinction is not always fixed. Normally an acid soil is preferred but some of the heaths, such as *E. carnea* x *darleyensis*, and their many cultivars, will tolerate neutral and even slightly alkaline soils. The range of flower and foliage colours available is very wide and needs consideration before you decide which to plant.

HEBE Scrophulariaceae

The genus *Hebe* contains about 100 species, some of which have many cultivars. Although a few are tender, or at least require some degree of protection from severe frosts, most have the ability to withstand wind and salt in the air. The flowers of most hebes are individually small but massed in inflorescences that have sequential opening times, spreading the flowering period in most cases throughout summer.

▼ **The leaves of the tall-growing *Hebe salicifolia* make the plant attractive even when it is not in flower.**

▲ **The hardy *Hebe* 'Great Orme' is a rather open shrub unless pruned hard.**

Leaf shape and size vary considerably between the species, and flower colour also ranges from blue, through mauves, purples and pinks, to white. Hebes will grow in most well–drained soils in full sun. They can be propagated from 2–4in (5–10cm) long leafy cuttings taken in late summer and placed in a sand and peat mixture for rooting.

H. salicifolia is one of the taller–growing species reaching about 10ft (3m), but the flowers are not particularly spectacular. 'Great Orme' is a hardy hybrid reaching about 5ft (1.5m) and bears a profusion of pinkish blue flowers. With such an enormous range of heights, from dwarf to tall, as well as leaf form and flower colour, the gardener should take the time to match plant site with species or cultivar characteristics.

HELENIUM Asteraceae

The most commonly grown species is *Helenium autumnale*, a hardy perennial flowering from summer to autumn, depending on the cultivar chosen, of which there are many. Colours range from yellow to coppery red, and early–flowering cultivars can often be made to flower again the same year by cutting back the first flowers as soon as they are over.

▲ Heliotrope (often known as cherry pie) produces clusters of blue/purple flowers.

HELIOTROPE Boraginaceae

The genus *Heliotropium* contains around 250 species, but the commonly cultivated form is *Heliotropium* x *hybridum* and there are many cultivars. Some heliotropes are tender annuals whilst others are shrubby. As a pot plant the common form grows to about 18in (45cm), but it can be trained to 24in (60cm) or more as a standard plant. The outdoor flowering period is from late spring to late autumn but potted plants can flower any time of the year. Fertile, well–drained soil in a sunny position is required. Cuttings can be taken in autumn or spring and should be about 3–4in (8–10cm) in length, taken from leafy sideshoots and kept at about 61–64°F (16–18°C) to root. They should be planted out in late spring. Seeds can also be sown in early spring in a heated propagator and then hardened off before planting out when large enough.

▲ The tender perennial *Ozothamnus rosmarinifolius* was once called *Helichrysum rosmarinifolium.*

HELICHRYSUM Asteraceae

Among the shrubby species is the familiar curry plant *H. italicum* (formerly *H. angustifolium*). The slightly tender *H. rosmarinifolium* with its profusion of white summer flowers is now correctly known as *Ozothamnus rosmarinifolius.*

   Helichrysum bracteatum used to be the scientific name for the commonly grown annual helichrysum, which comes in a range of cultivars with a variety of colour and form; it is now called *Bracteantha bracteata*. Other helichrysums are low–growing alpine plants, usually needing some protection in the winter.

HEMP AGRIMONY Asteraceae

The wild hemp agrimony of Europe and North Africa is *Eupatorium cannabinum*, a hardy herbaceous perennial growing to 4ft (1.2m). It flowers from mid–summer to autumn and a mass of inflorescences are produced, giving a reddish purple tinge to the plant. It can form an attractive addition to a wild garden if the site is carefully chosen so that the plant does not overshadow smaller plants.

▲ *Eupatorium cannabinum*, the European wild species of hemp agrimony, flowers from mid-summer to autumn.

HONESTY Brassicaceae

Lunaria annua, despite its Latin name, is a biennial or short–lived perennial from Europe, which flowers from spring to early summer. The fragrant flowers come in a range of shades from purple to white and the plant grows to around 30in (75cm) in height. It prefers a light, free–draining soil and some shade during part of the day. The round, moon–like seedpods from which the scientific name derives, contain several large seeds, which should be sown as soon as ripe. From late autumn to early spring the young plants should be set out where they are to flower. If winters are severe it is best to treat the plant as a biennial rather than rely on the old stools to grow out again in the spring. The taller *L. rediviva* grows to over 3ft (1m) and is a rather bushy, short–lived perennial with fragrant but paler flowers.

▲ The mauve flowers of honesty give way to seedpods that are used extensively for dried-flower arrangements.

North American agrimony

The North American *E. purpureum* grows to over 5ft (1.8m) and has paler, rose-purple flowers in late summer. It is also a hardy herbaceous perennial that will grow in most reasonably moist garden soils, in sun or partial shade. The plant is easily propagated by division and replanting during the dormant winter period, up to early spring. There are over 1,000 species in the genus.

▲ **The fragrant long-throated flowers of climbing honeysuckle are suited to long-tongued moths rather than butterflies.**

HONEYSUCKLE Caprifoliaceae

Although thought of as a flower for long–tongued moths, some butterflies will visit certain species of *Lonicera*. Several species are grown and many cultivars are available. There are shrubby species, such as *L. tartarica*, that have much shorter tubes to their flowers.

HYSSOP Lamiaceae

Although there are several subspecies and cultivars, there is only one species in this genus: *Hyssopus officinalis*, a native to the Mediterranean and Central Asian regions. It is a hardy herbaceous perennial growing to 20in (50cm) or more and can be used as a low hedge as well as a herb. If winter conditions are not too severe it is semi–evergreen and the leaves are strongly aromatic. The flowers are produced from mid–summer to autumn, and although the typical form has purple–blue flowers there are also pink and white forms. Cuttings about 2.5in (6cm) long can be taken from spring to early summer. These should be set out in a cold frame in a mixture of sand and peat for rooting. They should be planted out in autumn in their final positions.

Seeds can be sown in spring. The plant benefits from pruning, either to keep it at the required height – in the case of a hedge – or cut to within 2in (5cm) of the soil to prevent it becoming too woody at the base if it is growing in a herbaceous border.

ICE PLANT/SHOWY STONECROP
Crassulaceae

A summer to autumn–flowering plant, *Sedum spectabile* is particularly noted for attracting the more showy autumn butterflies. It should not be confused with *Cryophytum crystallinum*, which is also called the ice plant. *S. spectabile* has several cultivars, but there is still much to be said for growing the original plant with pinkish–red flowers and pale green leaves. It is a perennial, and easily propagated by division of the clumps. It prefers a well–drained soil in full sun.

There are other species in the genus *Sedum*, often called stonecrops, and many are drought tolerant. Because they are often smaller, they are most suited to rock gardens. The taller *S. telephium* does need a moisture–retentive, but well–drained, soil.

▼ **The ice plant is very attractive to butterflies in autumn.**

▲ **The scabious lookalike, *Jasione laevis*, flowers in mid-summer.**

JASIONE Campanulaceae

At first sight *Jasione laevis* (formerly *J. perennis*) when in bloom looks like a scabious, in the family *Dipsacaceae*. However, the detail of the flowers places it in an entirely different family although, confusingly, it is also known as the sheep's-bit scabious. It likes a sunny position in well-drained soil, and flowers during mid-summer.

KERRIA Rosaceae

Kerria japonica 'Simplex' is the name given to the single-flowered cultivar, but the majority of those grown are the double-flowered *K. japonica* 'Pleniflora' and other similar cultivars. If you can get it, the single is to be preferred. This spring-flowering shrub produces yellow flowers. It thrives in any garden soil and spreads by means of many suckering shoots, making it easily propagated by division.

KNAPWEED Asteraceae

There are several species in the genus *Centaurea* that are attractive to butterflies. They are predominantly European species although some are widely cultivated. Greater knapweed (*C. scabiosa*) is a herbaceous perennial growing to about 3ft (1m) and bears bright purple-red flowers from early to late summer. The black knapweed (*C. nigra*) also has purple-red flowers but is short, at around 24in (60cm), and flowers from mid-summer to autumn. The brown knapweed (*C. jacea*), and its frequent hybrids with *C. nigra*, bloom from late summer to autumn. All can be cultivated in the wild garden.

▶ **Black knapweed (*Centaurea nigra*) is a native European plant that can be cultivated.**

The cornflower

The most commonly grown species of knapweed is the cornflower (*C. cyanus*), which is an annual. It grows to 3ft (1m) in some forms, but dwarf cultivars are also available that do not reach much more than 12in (30cm). The flowers are borne from early summer through to autumn, and although typically blue, can also be pink or white. The plant grows in any fertile, well-drained soil provided it is given a sunny spot. Seeds can be sown in autumn to give an early start to the flowering season, or in succession in the spring to extend the flowering season. Many of the other 600 species in this genus are available.

LANTANA Verbenaceae

Although a frost–sensitive plant that forms an evergreen shrub up to 6ft (2m) tall, *Lantana camara* is also available to gardeners as a summer bedding plant. Its flowers come in a range of colours and are borne throughout the growing season. Butterflies find them very attractive. Lantana grows in most moist garden soils, in full sun. It should be noted that the attractive black berries that appear after the flowers are very poisonous, and the plant should not be grown where young children may eat the fruits.

▲ **Summer-flowering lavender will attract butterflies.**

▼ **Lantana flowers are a favourite with most butterflies.**

LAVENDER Lamiaceae

There are some 28 species of lavender, and quite a lot of confusion reigns over the names of some of the species, complicated further by the existence of many hybrids and cultivars. Although it is native to the Mediterranean region, English lavender (*Lavandula angustifolia*) is certainly worth growing. It is a hardy evergreen shrub that needs annual pruning to keep it from becoming too overgrown and woody. Light trimming should be done after flowering but the major cutting back should be carried out in spring. It is recommended that the plants be replaced every five years or so.

Lavender can be propagated easily: take cuttings 3–4in (8–10cm) long of ripened, non-flowering shoots in early autumn. These should be rooted in a peat and sand mixture in a cold frame and then planted out in spring. It is possible to take larger cuttings of some 6–8in (15–20cm) and set them out directly where they are to flower in late autumn, as long as the site is not too exposed or damp in the winter. Although the typical flower colour is blue, there are also cultivars with various purple, red and even white flowers, which are produced from summer to late autumn. Depending on the cultivar, plants can range in height when flowering from around 12in (30cm) to well over 3ft (1m), and this should be taken into account when choosing a particular site. All lavenders thrive in well-drained soil in a sunny position.

LIATRIS Asteraceae

Sometimes known as blazing star or gayfeather, *Liatris spicata* has pink–purple flower spikes up to 3ft (1m) tall in early autumn. It likes quite damp soil, as does *L. callilepis*, which will also tolerate poor soil. Both make attractive additions to the garden, and do not look like most other members of the aster family.

LIGULARIA Asteraceae

The ligularias are hardy herbaceous perennials, generally flowering from summer to early autumn, and most prefer a moist and partly shaded site. There are several species and cultivars available, and most grow to a height of 3ft (1m) or more and have yellow to orange flowers.

LILAC Oleaceae

Common lilac (*Syringa vulgaris*), and its many cultivars, is well known as a tough shrub or small tree that flowers in late spring and early summer, and comes in a wide range of colours. Most named cultivars are grafted onto a stock which may be a lilac itself, or a privet, which is less prone to troublesome suckering. Although a tolerant plant, the lilac prefers a well–drained soil in full sun. To attract butterflies a single–flowered cultivar should be chosen. The Canadian hybrids (for Canada is where they were first raised) are also worth growing for their masses of flowers and excellent scent.

LOBELIA Campanulaceae

The familiar bedding and trailing lobelias come in a number of different cultivars and are either ascribed to the species *Lobelia erinus* or simply given their cultivar name. Although technically tender perennials they are normally grown as annuals and are available to gardeners during spring. If carefully fed and watered they can flower from spring through to autumn. These plants have short tubes and their nectar is generally available to butterflies, but the taller–growing species, such as the cardinal plant (*L. cardinalis*), a red perennial for pond edges, are less suitable.

▼ **Trailing lobelias are more attractive to butterflies than the species with larger tubes to the flowers.**

French lavender

The other commonly grown form of lavender is French lavender (*L. stoechus*), which has very truncated inflorescences that some find more attractive than the English lavenders. There are many cultivars available and although the typical form has purple flowers and grows to about 24in (60cm), there are many variations in height, vigour and flower colour. The flowering period is rather shorter than that of English lavenders, lasting from early to mid-summer in most cultivars.

LUCERNE/ALFALFA Papilionaceae

Although originally a wild plant there are now many cultivated forms used in agriculture, some of which may be the true *Medicago sativa*, while others are hybrids with improved characteristics. The plant is a perennial that puts down a strong and extensive root system and will last for five years or more. The flowers are usually violet and can be quite attractive, although it is more a plant for the wild garden than the herbaceous border.

LYSIMACHIA Primulaceae

Several species and a number of cultivars of *Lysimachia* are grown in gardens. *L. punctata* has bright yellow flowers and *L. clethroides* has white flowers; both species carry flowering spikes 6in (15cm) or more long from summer to early autumn. They can be a little invasive, but are nevertheless good border plants. Creeping jenny (*L. nummularia*) is a trailing plant that can be used as ground cover, and which produces yellow flowers in summer. All prefer soil that is moist, but will tolerate quite dry conditions.

▼ Garden loosestrife (*Lysimachia punctata*) is a tough, spreading herbaceous perennial.

▲ Low outdoor winter temperatures can influence flower development, and may promote doubleness or abnormal blooms, as with this *Calendula officinalis*.

MARIGOLDS Asteraceae

A clear distinction must be made between African and French marigolds (species and cultivars of *Tagetes*) and the cultivars of the pot marigold (*Calendula officinalis*), although the single forms of both are attractive to butterflies. Double forms are to be avoided because the crowded petals make it difficult for the butterfly to reach the nectar. All marigolds can be grown from seed or bought in as young plants for bedding out in late spring. A moist soil, in full sun, is preferred.

MARJORAM Lamiaceae

Ordinary marjoram, often called origano (*Origanum vulgare*) is a hardy perennial found wild in the UK and Europe. It grows to a height of 12–18in (30–45cm) and produces rose–purple flowers from mid to late summer. Pot marjoram is another species (*O. onites*), which grows to about 12in (30cm), with mauve to white flowers, and is a slightly tender sub–shrub that needs a little bit of protection in cold winters. Sweet majoram (*O. majorana*) is a hardy sub–shrub growing to about 24in (60cm) with flowers ranging from mauve through pink to white, which are produced from early summer to autumn.

Marjorams need a well-drained soil in full sun and should be pruned back by about two-thirds before they die back in winter. Cuttings

can be taken from basal shoots, about 2–3in (5–7cm) long, in mid–spring, and set out in a peat and sand mixture. They can also be propagated by seeds sown in a propagator in late winter for planting out in early summer, or directly in the soil in late spring.

MEXICAN ORANGE BLOSSOM Rutaceae

Choisya ternata and its yellow–leaved cultivars are shrubby evergreens that are hardy in most places but do benefit from a protected site in colder areas. They will grow in most well–drained soils. The ordinary green form will reach a height of around 6ft (2m), rather less for the variegated ones. White flowers are produced mostly in spring but a few may appear from time to time throughout summer and autumn.

MICHAELMAS DAISY Asteraceae

There are some 500 species, and a large range of cultivars, in the *Aster* genus; the ordinary michaelmas daisy is ascribed to *A. novi-belgii*. Most are typically autumn–flowering. Depending on the cultivar they can range from dwarf forms at 8–16in (20–40cm) to tall ones at 2–4ft (60–120cm). There are many colours available from red and pink to purple and blue. They require a well–drained fertile soil – but not one that dries out during the critical flowering period – in an open, sunny position. The tall cultivars generally need supporting to prevent them falling over in windy weather. It is usual to cut down the stems after flowering is complete. If good flowering plants over many years are to be encouraged, regular division is required – to prevent the centres of the clumps from deteriorating. This should be done in early spring, keeping only the parts of the plants that are healthy. With unusual cultivars that are in short supply it is possible to take single shoot cuttings in spring, for rooting in a peat and sand mixture before planting out.

▶ **Michaelmas daisies are autumn-flowering butterfly plants that come in a wide range of heights to suit any position in the border.**

MIGNONETTE Resedaceae

The wild mignonette (*Reseda lutea*) of the UK and Europe is a biennial with a mass of greenish–yellow flowers produced from early summer till autumn. It grows to anything from 12–28in (30–70cm) in height. Weld (*R. luteola*) is a more vigorous plant growing up to 5ft (1.5m) and flowers over the same period. Both of these species are more for the wild garden, on chalky or neutral soil, than for the ornamental garden. The species usually found in gardens is *R. odorata* from North Africa.

It is usually grown as a hardy annual but may survive for several years in more favourable spots; it reaches a height of around 28in (70cm). The whitish–yellow flowers are more attractive than those of the former two species as they have bright orange–yellow stamens, and there are also various cultivars that are more brightly coloured. It has a long flowering season from early summer to late autumn. It likes a sunny position in a rich, well–drained soil, preferably one that is chalky. Mignonette can be grown from seed sown directly into the flowering position during spring. Alternatively, sow seed in a propagator in autumn or late winter for hardening off and planting out in spring.

MILKWEED/BUTTERFLY WEED Asclepiadaceae

There are several different species of milkweed, belonging to the genus *Asclepias*. The flowers are specially adapted for pollination by butterflies. Sometimes while the butterflies are feeding, one of their legs can become temporarily trapped in these flowers; small species may have to struggle a little to get away. However, it does not usually deter them from visiting the next flower on the plant. *A. tuberosa* is a hardy perennial which flowers in summer and is certainly worth planting in well–drained soil in full sun. The tender *A. curassavica* will be familiar to visitors of tropical butterfly houses, but has also gained popularity as a summer pot or even bedding plant, and it makes an attractive addition to any herbaceous border. It can be propagated easily by seed; just sow early in the year in a heated propagator.

Did you know?

All the milkweed species are food plants for caterpillars of the monarch and some other Danaid butterflies. Where these butterflies occur naturally, growing milkweed can help to increase local numbers over the warmer months.

◀ **The tender milkweed (*Asclepias curassavica*) is becoming a popular medium-height summer plant in temperate regions.**

MINT Lamiaceae

Many species, hybrids and cultivars of *Mentha* are cultivated, some as herbs and others for their variegated leaves or unusual scents. Butterflies will visit mints but these plants are usually grown for other reasons, and it is well known that some forms can be quite invasive. The strongly scented penny–royal (*M. pulegium*) is said to keep ants away, but we have not found this to be true always.

PEARL EVERLASTING Asteraceae

This herbaceous perennial, *Anaphalis margaritacea*, flowers in late summer and has grey foliage that adds interest for the gardener in the earlier part of the year. There are a few cultivars available and other species in the genus are also grown.

PETUNIA Solanaceae

There are very many cultivars belonging to *Petunia* x *hybrida* and the second part of the Latin name is often dropped in labels and books. Although really perennial plants they are usually grown as annuals, flowering in spring and summer. They prefer a light, well–drained soil in a sunny position. There are many different colours available and plants are usually bought in as well–developed seedlings for use in beds, pots and hanging baskets. They are not particularly attractive to the smaller species of butterflies but may be visited by those with long tongues.

PHLOX Polemoniaceae

The genus contains something over 60 species with a variety of life forms from half–hardy annuals and alpine plants, to hardy shrubs. *Phlox drummondii* is one of the two most commonly cultivated species. It is a half–hardy annual with

▶ **The wild primrose is a favourite spring flower.**

the common forms growing to about 16in (40cm) and can be grown in any fertile, well-drained soil in an open sunny position. The normal flowering period is from mid–summer to autumn and there are many cultivars available which vary in height and colour – these range from red and purple through pink to white. Seedlings started in trays can be set out in late spring, but for really early flowering it is best to sow the seed in a heated propagator during autumn, for planting out during the early spring.

The other commonly cultivated species is *P. paniculata*, which is a herbaceous perennial from North America. It flowers from mid–summer to autumn. There are many cultivars available ranging from violet, red and pink to pure white, and with heights from 18 to 48in (45 to 120cm). They like a fertile, moisture–retentive but well–drained soil in a sunny or only partially shaded spot. The height and weight of the flowers usually means that staking is necessary and the plants are usually cut down in late autumn.

Propagation is by 1.5–2in (4–5cm) cuttings from the base of the plants taken when growth has just started in spring. They are rooted in a peat and sand mixture for planting out when large enough. It is sometimes recommended to take cuttings of sections of root rather than stem, to avoid possible trouble with stem eelworm, which can be a serious pest. Root cuttings can be taken at any time, but late winter is preferred, with the use of a propagator. Very small pieces can be taken but it may be over a year before the plants are large enough to plant out.

PRIMROSE Primulaceae

The *Primula* genus has some 500 species in it and these range from hardy to half-hardy perennials, some retaining their leaves all winter whilst others are deciduous. The common wild primrose (*P. vulgaris*) has yellow flowers produced in spring. They are low–growing plants that only reach about 6in (15cm) and must be provided with a moist soil that does not dry out during

▲ **The cowslip does not thrive in areas that are intensively farmed.**

the growing season. The site can be in full sun or partially shaded and any good garden soil is suitable. If seeds are sown they must be fresh but it is more usual to divide existing clumps, as the seedlings take many months to get established to a good size for planting out.

Did you know?

The term 'polyanthus' is used to describe garden forms that are mostly hybrids between the common primrose and the cowslip (*Primula veris*). They come in a wide range of colours and some are suitable for growing in the garden, but it should be noted that many are only suitable for indoor culture or for growing outdoors in the warmer months.

▲ **Let a privet hedge flower to attract butterflies.**

PRIVET Oleaceae

Although thought of as primarily a hedging plant, the various species and cultivars of *Ligustrum* will produce flowers if not kept too tightly clipped. These flowers will, even on the variegated forms, attract butterflies so that if you do not mind a somewhat unkempt hedge with a sunny aspect, they are worth considering.

PURPLE LOOSESTRIFE Lythraceae

Lythrum salicaria grows to a height of about 5ft (1.5m) and has dramatic tall spikes of purple-red flowers from mid–summer to early autumn. *L. virgatum* is only about 3ft (1m) tall. Both species have many cultivars, both are hardy herbaceous perennials, and both are quite tolerant of conditions, but obviously a sunny border is preferable if the aim is to attract butterflies.

RED CLOVER Papilionaceae

Red clover (*Trifolium pratense*) is available in several cultivars. It is a hardy, spreading perennial that can be used in a wild meadow or, if kept under control, with other plants in a sunny garden position. White clover (*T. repens*) and its cultivars can be similarly grown.

RHODODENDRON/AZALEA Ericaceae

There are very many species and cultivars available within the genus *Rhododendron*, and most prefer a well–drained acid soil. They nearly all flower in spring and early summer, and may be visited by butterflies attracted to their brightly coloured flowers, especially early in the season when other flowering plants are not yet in bloom. Because of their size, large shrubs are not to be recommended for the smaller butterfly garden.

◀ **Purple loosestrife (*Lythrum salicaria*) is a dramatic butterfly plant, growing to some 5ft (1.5m) in height.**

◁ **Rhododendrons are not specially adapted for butterflies, but some cultivars may be visited during spring.**

ROCKCRESS Brassicaceae

The species usually cultivated is *Arabis alpina* subsp. *caucasica* (which has also been known as *A. caucasica* and *A. albida*). There are several cultivars available and the single-flowered ones are to be preferred. They are spring-flowering perennials and like a very well-drained soil in full sun – which makes them most suitable for dry walls and banks.

ROSEBAY WILLOWHERB Onagraceae

Suitable for the very wild garden or the back of a border, *Epilobium angustifolium* and its cultivars are herbaceous perennials that can reach more than 6ft (2m) in height. They are particularly showy with their crimson or white flowers.

ROSEMARY Lamiaceae

Both a herb and a decorative plant, *Rosmarinus officinalis* comes in many different cultivars, some of which can grow as tall as 6ft (2m). The flowers, produced mainly in spring but often at other times up to early autumn, can be mauve and blue through to white. Forms previously known as *R. lavandulaceus*, with a low, spreading habit, are now considered to be *R. officinalis* Prostratus Group. These appear to be rather less hardy, but can usefully be grown to cover the ground in sheltered spots.

ROUND-HEADED RAMPION Campanulaceae

Phyteuma tenerum is a wild plant of chalky grassland, found naturally in the south of the UK and throughout Europe. It is a deep-rooted perennial, flowering from mid to late summer, growing up to 20in (50cm) in height, and bearing deep violet flowers. It is sometimes grown in gardens, along with several other species in the genus, some of which are dwarf rockery plants.

RUNNER BEAN Papilionaceae

Primarily grown as a vegetable, the runner bean (*Phaseolus coccineus*), and its cultivars, can make an attractive climbing plant in its own right. Although its flowers are not adapted for butterflies they may nevertheless be visited, so the plants could be grown in the ornamental rather than the kitchen garden.

SAINFOIN Papilionaceae

Widely planted as an agricultural crop, sainfoin (*Onobrychis vicifolia*) is a perennial that produces dense masses of pinkish-red flowers over summer. When found wild it has a preference for slightly alkaline grassland and could be grown in similar conditions in a wild garden, although the flowers are more adapted for bees than for butterflies.

SALLOW/WILLOW Salicaceae

The genus *Salix* contains around 500 species, and many hybrids and cultivated forms exist. They are hardy deciduous trees and shrubs that can reach very large sizes, and this needs to be considered before selecting one for planting in the garden. Most large species are not recommended for growing near to houses. The main value of the genus to the butterfly gardener is that the plants in it produce flowers early in spring, usually on leafless stems, so that butterflies emerging from hibernation early can make use of them when not many flowers are available.

The sallow (*Salix caprea*), also known as goat willow and pussy willow, is a plant native to the UK and Europe. It can be vigorous, growing to 45ft (15m), so it cannot really be recommended for the average garden in the wild form although there are various cultivars which are more desirable. If kept under control it may be useful as part of a hedge in damp positions. The woolly willow (*S. lanata*) is, by contrast, a slow-growing shrub reaching only 4ft (1.3m) or so in height, and is even recommended for larger rock gardens.

The osier (*S. viminalis*) has several cultivars with coloured stems, which make it an attractive addition to the garden during winter. The flowers are borne in late spring, and like all willows it prefers a moist soil. *S. gracilistyla* and its cultivars, from Japan and Korea, grow to about 8ft (2.5m), and bear 2in (5cm) long red and grey male catkins which turn to yellow as the stamens expand.

▼ **Although generally wind-pollinated, the flowers of the *Salix* species also have nectaries that may provide early season food for butterflies.**

Did you know?

All willows are easily propagated from cuttings, some 10–14in (25–35cm) long, of firm wood taken in the dormant winter period. Set these cuttings out directly in a nursery bed to root before transferring to their final position when established.

SAW-WORT Asteraceae

This is a wild herbaceous perennial growing mainly on moist soils over chalk or limestone, and widely distributed throughout the UK and Europe through to Asia and North Africa. The margins of the leaves bear fine, bristle-tipped teeth. The Latin name is *Serratula tinctoria* and this and a few related species are sometimes grown in gardens. The florets are normally reddish purple but very occasionally white, and they are produced from mid-summer to early autumn.

SCABIOUS Dipsacaceae

The name scabious is used for plants in several different genera, and all of them are attractive to butterflies. Sweet scabious (*Scabiosa atropurpurea*) from southern Europe is a hardy annual reaching about 3ft (1m) when bearing its flowers from mid-summer to autumn. In the wild form these are dark crimson, but many cultivars exist with flowers in shades of blue, pink and white, as well as some shorter ones reaching only about 18in (45cm) in height. In contrast, *S. caucasica* is a hardy perennial reaching about 24in (60cm), again with many cultivars in colours from lavender blue through mauve to white. The small scabious (*S. columbaria*) is a wild plant of the UK and Europe, where it produces its blue-violet flowers from mid-summer to autumn.

Basal cuttings – some 2in (5cm) long – of the perennial species can be taken in spring, and should be set into a peat and sand mixture. Grow them on and plant them out in autumn or the following

▲ **There are many cultivated forms of scabious grown in gardens and they are generally easy to propagate.**

▲ *Senecio confusus* **(seen here with a zebra heliconid) is a tender plant that is attractive to butterflies.**

spring. The annual species can be propagated by seeds sown in spring or, with some protection, in autumn. Perennial species should be divided every three or four years to maintain vigour.

The plant that grows wild in the UK and Europe, which is known as the field scabious, belongs to another genus *Knautia arvensis*. It has blue–violet flowers from mid–summer to mid–autumn and there are various cultivated members of the same genus. Devil's–bit scabious (*Succisa pratensis*) is from yet another genus and also grows wild in the UK and Europe. The mauve–purplish flowers are borne from early summer to late autumn.

SENECIO Asteraceae

The genus *Senecio* has around 3,000 species, and among the many cultivated species there are annuals, herbaceous perennials, shrubs and succulents. Many of these would be able to attract butterflies. One that is commonly grown is the lax shrub sometimes called *Senecio laxifolis*, but which is now properly called *Brachyglottis* (Dunedin Group) 'Sunshine'. To make matters worse the plant is similar to *Brachyglottis greyi* (formerly *Senecio greyi*) and the two are frequently mislabelled. This is not too much of a problem since both have bright yellow flowers borne in masses from early to late summer. The bright orange blossoms of *Senecio confusus* are about 1in (2cm) in diameter and are borne in small clusters.

▲ **Common ragwort (*Senecio jacobaea*) looks attractive but is considered a weed and poisonous to livestock.**

⏶ **Although considered a flower pollinated by wasps, the snowberry may attract butterflies to its nectar.**

SNOWBERRY Caprifoliaceae

Symphoricarpos albus is a suckering shrub with small pinkish–green flowers from mid–summer to early autumn. They give rise to round white berries later in the season. The flowers are pollinated by wasps mainly, but if in a sunny position they may attract butterflies. There are several cultivars, some more suitable for hedging than the very rampant original species, which can grow to over 6ft (2m) and be rather invasive. The coral berry or Indian currant (*S. orbiculatus*) has pink to purple berries.

SOAPWORT Caryophyllaceae

Saponaria officinalis is called soapwort because its sap can act like soap. It is a hardy perennial that can grow to almost 3ft (1m), and produces pink flowers from mid–summer to early autumn. It grows wild in the UK, Europe and Asia, and as an introduced species in North America. In cultivation it has largely been replaced by double cultivars. Several other species and their cultivars are also grown.

⏶ **Several painted ladies enjoy the dense pink flower clusters of *Spiraea* 'Anthony Waterer'.**

SPIRAEA Rosaceae

Many species and cultivars in the genus *Spiraea* are available in cultivation. The plant formerly known as *S.* x *bumalda* is now known as *S. japonica* 'Bumalda'. It is a hardy deciduous shrub reaching over 4ft (1.2m), and bears masses of pink flowers in summer.

▲ **The strawberry tree (*Arbutus unedo*) can provide nectar for late autumn butterflies prior to hibernation.**

STRAWBERRY TREE Ericaceae

Although several species in the genus *Arbutus* are cultivated, the name strawberry tree is usually given to *A. unedo* and its cultivars. This is a slightly tender evergreen shrub that can reach 16ft (5m) in favourable spots. The white or pinkish flowers are borne in hanging clusters in mid–autumn to early winter, and can provide nectar for butterflies that are about to hibernate. The common name derives from the strawberry–like fruits that stay on the tree for a year or so.

SUNFLOWER Asteraceae

The familiar annual sunflower is *Helianthus annuus* and there are several cultivars available for sowing in spring, but some may be too tall for planting in the average flowerbed. There are also several other perennial species in the genus *Helianthus* that are good garden plants, mostly flowering in summer and autumn in sunny positions with well–drained soil. Mostly the flowers are yellow or orange but some forms with red blooms are also available.

SWEET ROCKET Brassicaceae

Hesperis matronalis is the most commonly grown member of a genus with some 30 species. It is a hardy herbaceous perennial from southern Europe and western Asia, and grows to about 3ft (1m) in height. There are various cultivars available in colours from purple and mauve to white, borne in early summer, and noted for their evening fragrance. The plant prefers a well–drained but moist soil in a sunny position. Roots can be divided over the dormant winter period and self–sown seedlings are common but will not come true for the named cultivars. Collected seeds can be sown in spring in trays, and the seedlings set out into a nursery bed in early summer. Transplant them in the autumn to their flowering positions.

SWEET WILLIAM Caryophyllaceae

The genus *Dianthus* has some 300 species of evergreen perennials and annuals. The cultivated sweet william (*D. barbatus*), from Eastern Europe, is a short–lived perennial with many cultivars. The plant is often grown as a biennial from seed sown early in the year to give plants that can be moved to their flowering positions in late autumn. Sweet williams are generally in the height range of 12–24in (30–60cm), and come in a range of colours from red to pink, some with complex marking patterns. The flowers are produced from early to mid–summer. If seeds are sown in a propagator in early spring it is possible to grow them on rapidly so that they flower in the first year. The plants prefer a well–drained, slightly alkaline soil in a sunny position. Unless seeds are required it is best to remove the flowering stems as soon as they are over, to encourage good flowering in the next season. The maiden pink (*D. deltoides*) flowers from early summer through to autumn, and is available with flowers from red to white.

TEASEL Dipsacaceae

Teasel (*Dipsacus fullonum*) is a herbaceous perennial that grows to around 6ft (2m), although it is a wild plant in the UK, Europe and elsewhere, it is usually grown as an ornamental plant, and occasionally as a crop. The dense head of rose–purple flowers is borne from mid to late summer and will attract the longer–tongued butterflies. Most gardeners grow a few teasel plants to provide seeds for small birds later in the year, or for use in dried–flower arrangements.

THISTLE Asteraceae

There are many types of thistle belonging to several different genera. The spear thistle (*Cirsium vulgare*) grows wild in the UK and Europe and has flowering stems up to 5ft (1.5m) high. Pink–purple flowers appear from mid–summer to late autumn. The creeping thistle (*C. arvense*) can be a serious weed due to its creeping roots, which throw up flowering stalks at intervals. These tend to be shorter than those of the spear thistle, but its purplish flowers appear at the same time. Our lady's milk thistle (*Silybum marianum*) is widespread in many countries.

It is an annual to biennial plant, flowering from early summer to early autumn. Almost any soil in an open, sunny site is suitable but it is generally grown at the back of a border, or in the wild garden, due to its height of around 4ft (1.2m).

▼ **Thistles – of which there are many – are a sure attraction for butterflies like the small tortoiseshells.**

The faintly fragrant flowers are deep violet. Seeds can be sown in autumn or spring if it is being grown as an annual. A couple of other species in the *Silybum* genus are also grown as garden plants.

The Scotch or cotton thistle (*Onopordum acanthium*) is a member of a genus with some 40 species.

Its striking growth, to almost 6ft (2m), once seen is not likely to be forgotten. It is a stately herbaceous perennial, but cannot really be recommended for a small garden. It grows in any rich soil, and will stand some shade for part of the day. It flowers from mid–summer to early autumn. Like all thistles it can self-seed extensively, or the seeds can be started in a propagator in early spring for hardening off and planting out in early summer.

THRIFT/SEA PINK Plumbaginaceae

Armeria maritima is a native plant of the UK and Europe, and it is typically found close to the sea. In the garden, however, it can be planted in any well–drained soil in full sun. Several cultivars are available with flower colours either darker or paler than the basic pink of the species, and these appear during summer. Several other species in the genus are also cultivated.

THYME Lamiaceae

There are several hundred species and very many cultivars in the genus *Thymus*. The ordinary herb thyme is *T. vulgaris*, while wild thyme (and its many garden cultivars) is *T. serpyllum*. Most thymes are low–growing, and some are chosen specially for use as ground cover. All are aromatic hardy perennials with flower colours that range from deep red and purple, through to lilac, pink and white depending on the cultivar. Most are summer–flowering.

TOADFLAX Scrophulariaceae

Several species in the genus *Linaria* are cultivated, one of the commonest being *L. purpurea* and its cultivars. This is a hardy perennial growing to a height of 3ft (1m) or more, with slender spikes of

▲ *Verbena bonariensis* **is a tall-growing species that can reach 39in (1m) or more in height.**

violet or pink flowers from mid–summer to early autumn. Pale toadflax (*L. repens*) is rarely cultivated but is a wild plant of the UK and Europe with mainly pale violet or white flowers, and a preference for slightly alkaline soils. Ivy–leaved toadflax (*Cymbalaria muralis*) grows wild on old walls and has given rise to several cultivars for garden use.

TORMENTIL Rosaceae

This widely distributed wild perennial plant of the UK, Europe, North Africa and elsewhere is *Potentilla erecta*, with yellow flowers borne in summer. Although it can be cultivated, there are many other species and cultivars in the genus *Potentilla* that make much more attractive garden plants. They cover the range from hardy annuals and perennials to both tall and low–growing shrubs, many of which flower from early summer to late autumn.

TRAVELLER'S JOY/OLD MAN'S BEARD
Ranunculaceae

The wild *Clematis vitalba* of the UK, Europe and North Africa, can be grown in gardens. It carries greenish–white flowers from mid to late summer. It has, however, been largely replaced by many other species, hybrids and cultivars. Although butterflies may on occasion visit the flowers of this plant, it is more likely that you will see regular appearances of bees and flies. In wild garden hedges there is a place for traveller's joy.

VALERIAN Valerianaceae

Common valerian (*Valeriana officinalis*) is a herbaceous perennial from the UK and Europe, and grows to about 4.5ft (1.3m) in wet places, and somewhat smaller on dry calcareous grassland. Its pinkish–white flowers are borne from early to late summer. It is not a plant that is generally grown in gardens, although some other members of the genus are.

The plant that is commonly grown, and which also escapes and grows wild on walls and other dry places, is red valerian (*Centranthus ruber*). This grows to around 3ft (1m) in height and the flowers, although typically red, may also be pink and even white. They are produced from early to late summer in the wild and even into autumn in the garden. Seeds can be sown from spring to early summer, either in a seed bed or directly where they are to flower. Self–seeding is common. Plants should be moved when quite small as they resent disturbance when large.

VERBENA Verbenaceae

The common garden verbena (*V.* x *hybrida*) has many cultivars, some of which are dwarf at 6in (15cm), whilst others grow up to 18in (45cm). Colours vary from blue, through mauve, red and pink to white. Most are propagated by seed rather than by cuttings, although these can be taken if a propagator is available. Of the 250 or so species in the genus several are in cultivation. One of the most striking and attractive to butterflies is *Verbena bonariensis* from South America with flowering stems to 5ft (1.5m) bearing masses of rose–lavender flowers in the crowded inflorescences. The plant is generally a short–lived perennial in mild areas and easily propagated by seed which, if sown early in the year in a propagator, can produce flowering plants in the first year. Cuttings of young shoots in early spring can be taken for rooting in a heated propagator. Division of the roots can be attempted a little later with any clumps that have overwintered successfully.

▲ *Viburnum x burkwoodii* **has strongly scented flowers.**

▲ **Cultivated pansies flower profusely in spring, seen here with pale blue forget-me-nots.**

VIBURNUM Caprifoliaceae

There are many good flowering shrubs in the genus *Viburnum*, and if room permits it is a good idea to plant some. *V.* x *burkwoodii* is an evergreen hybrid with particularly strongly scented flowers borne in dense, rounded clusters in spring. Other species flower in winter, which is of little use to adult butterflies, while summer–flowering species and cultivars also exist.

VIOLA/PANSY Violaceae

Most of the garden pansies now grown are cultivars, and there are many of them. Some flower from early summer to early autumn, in many different colours, while others flower from late autumn to spring. Butterflies may visit pansies but they are not particularly attracted to them.

There are also many species of the genus *Viola* available. The wild pansy of the UK, Europe and elsewhere is *V. tricolour* and is part parent to many of the garden cultivars. It flowers from late spring to early autumn and itself can come in a range of colour combinations. The sweet violet (*V. odorata*) usually produces its scented flowers from late winter to early spring.

WALLFLOWER Brassicaceae

The common wallflower, which grows both in gardens and wild on old walls, used to be known as *Cheiranthus cheiri*, but is now called *Erysimum cheiri*. The yellow to orange–red flowers are produced in spring and early summer, and several cultivars are available which vary in height from 8–24in (20–60cm). The plant needs a well–drained, sunny position on slightly alkaline soil for best growth. Seeds can be sown in the open in early summer for growing on and planting out in late autumn to flower the next spring. The Siberian wallflower (*Erysimum* x *allionii*) has orange flowers from late spring to mid–summer, and again several cultivars are available.

▲ **Orange wallflowers (*Erysimum cheiri*) in a mixed spring bed.**

WAYFARING TREE Caprifoliaceae

The wayfaring tree (*Viburnum lantana*) – actually a deciduous shrub – is native to the UK, Europe and elsewhere, mainly on alkaline soils. It produces masses of creamy–white flowers from late spring to early summer. This is slightly earlier than the guelder rose (*V. opulus*), which is more frequently seen on damper soils. Some of the many species and cultivars of *Viburnum* available are evergreen; there are hybrids, also, with varying growth habits and flowering times, making viburnums an interesting and diverse group of plants for the gardener.

WHITE DEAD-NETTLE Lamiaceae

Lamium album is a native plant of the UK, Europe and elsewhere, and is available for growing in gardens mostly as cultivars. It is a creeping herbaceous perennial familiar along roadsides and in waste places where its whorls of white flowers are borne from early summer right through to the winter.

Other species and cultivars from the genus *Lamium* are also grown in gardens, but it must be said that the insects visiting their flowers are mainly bees.

WILD PEAR Rosaceae

The wild pear of the UK, Europe and elsewhere is *Pyrus communis*; the familiar pear fruits are some of the cultivars of this species. Masses of flowers appear in spring, with the exact time depending on the cultivar – as well as the weather. If this coincides with the appearance of overwintering butterflies, they may well take advantage of the blossom. But most people plant pears for their fruit.

WISTERIA Papilionaceae

There are many cultivars among the various species of *Wisteria*, which are deciduous spring–flowering climbers. An occasional second flush is produced in summer. They come in various shades of blue, purple, pink and white, and prefer a well–drained but sunny site. Not thought of generally as butterfly flowers, they may provide nectar to some longer–tongued species early in the year.

YARROW Asteraceae

Although the common yarrow (*Achillea millefolium*) is a common weed in the UK there are many improved cultivars that are available to grow as garden plants. They are perennials with a long flowering period from spring to autumn, and come in shades of yellow and red as well as the basic white. They like a well–drained soil in full sun but are generally quite tough plants and well worth planting. Many other species of *Achillea* are available as garden plants and there is considerable variation in height, from very dwarf to over 3ft (1m), so it is worth taking care that you get a species and/or cultivar that is suitable for the site you have.

ZINNIA Asteraceae

Zinnias are half–hardy annuals grown from seed, or young plants bought in, for late spring planting and summer flowering. Two species are commonly cultivated: *Zinnia angustifolia* and *Z. elegans*, both with a range of cultivars and flower colours. Choose the single forms for butterflies.

Common butterflies that visit gardens can vary widely all over the world, despite the similarities in the plants that attract them. This is because physical barriers – such as oceans or mountain ranges – have led to various butterfly species evolving in isolation in different parts of the world. This section examines the very different butterflies of Australia and New Zealand, Europe and North America in temperate climates.

Common garden butterflies

Butterflies that visit gardens

THE PLANTS we choose to grow in our gardens have their origins in many different countries, and it is true that there is a high degree of similarity in the plants that are to be found in all temperate–zone gardens throughout the world. It is a very different story, however, with the common butterflies that visit the gardens. They can vary widely.

It has always been easy to transport seeds and other plant–propagation material from one country to another. Until relatively recently it has not been easy to transport most live butterflies in the same way, regardless of the stages of the life cycles. Although nowadays butterflies can be transported easily from one country to another, extensive legislation essentially prevents the liberation of any species, subspecies or strains of species that do not occur naturally in a country. Butterfly gardeners across the globe can therefore have very similar gardens, yet they will attract totally different species of butterfly.

There is still some confusion over grouping butterflies into families of related genera and species. The schemes used in old books are likely to differ from those found in the latest works on the subject. So, to avoid further confusion we have chosen not to use the family names. Instead we are using English terms that indicate appropriate relationships.

As is the situation with plants, some of the Latin names used here are new, so you are unlikely to find them in older references. Where this causes confusion we apologize, and hope that the English name used will avoid confusion. It is not the purpose of this chapter to act as a butterfly identification guide. The descriptions given of the adult butterflies are intended only as an indication of their appearance and should not be taken as strictly accurate for identification purposes.

Readers should consult an identification guide to ensure complete accuracy. Lists of butterfly species found in your local area may be available. Unfortunately, we cannot include pictures of all the species, or all the varieties of forms mentioned for identification or comparative purposes.

◀ **Some day-flying moths, such as this European six-spot burnet, can be confused with butterflies.**

Directory of common garden butterflies

Australia and New Zealand

ALTHOUGH THERE are temperate regions in both Australia and New Zealand, the number of butterflies found in the two countries is markedly different, due both to the overall size of the countries, and the greater range of conditions and habitats found in Australia. In terms of Australian fauna it has long been accepted that there are three major faunal regions, although the exact boundaries between them cannot be precisely defined. The Torresian zone includes northern Australia, the eastern parts of Queensland and the north-eastern parts of New South Wales. The Eyrean zone is largely defined as being the more arid parts of Australia, receiving normally less than 20in (50cm) of rain per year. The Bassian zone covers the remaining southern parts of Australia. The few Australian species that have been selected as being reasonably comparable to those found in Europe, the UK and the USA are from the eastern parts of the Bassian zone.

Of over 300 butterfly species and many subspecies, fewer than a third are members of the hesperiids (skippers) and slightly more are members of the lycaenids (blues and their relatives). Some are difficult for the casual butterfly gardener to distinguish between, but we have included a few that we think are more likely to turn up in gardens.

Australian Butterflies

AUSTRALIAN PAINTED LADY
Vanessa kershawi

Group: Nymphalids

This species was at one time considered to be a subspecies of the painted lady (*V. cardui*) but is now considered to be a separate species on the basis of blue centres to the black spots on the hindwings and differences found upon close examination of the male genitalia. The painted lady is only found in the south-west of Australia, but the Australian painted lady occurs throughout the country and in New Zealand.

Both the front and hindwings have a complex pattern of black over an orange-red base and the front wings have several white spots towards the tip. The underside of the front wing is similar to the upperside but the underside of the hindwing is complexly patterned in brown and yellow making the butterfly difficult to spot when resting among foliage. Depending on the climate they may be on the wing all the year round but only in the warmer months in the south. There are mass migrations towards the south in the period from early spring to early summer. The eggs are laid singly on the leaves of a number of different plant species but not so many as have been recorded for the painted lady.

Plants in the family Asteraceae are mostly used, including the Scotch thistle (*Onopordum acanthium*) and species of *Artemesia*. Wild plants used include *Ammobium alatum*, *Helichrysum bracteatum* and *Helipterum roseum*.

The mature caterpillars are generally dark but can be greenish-yellow and have many branched spines, and lightish stripes along the sides. Caterpillars mostly feed at night and shelter during the day in loose tents of leaves or near the ground. The chrysalids hang by their tails from underneath stalks of the food plant or elsewhere.

▲ **The European cabbage or small white is an attractive butterfly, but as an introduced species is considered a pest in Australia.**

CABBAGE WHITE *Pieris rapae*

Group: Pierids

This cabbage white is also known as the small white in other parts of the world. It is one of the commonest butterflies wherever plants from the Brassica family are grown across the globe. It arrived in Australia, probably from New Zealand, in 1937. More detailed information about this butterfly is given in the section on European and UK butterflies.

CAPER WHITE *Anaphaeis java*

Group: Pierids

Both males and females are very similar, as they possess white uppersides with black margins to the wings and some white spotting on the black. The females have a small dark mark towards the centre of the wings. The underside of the front wings is similar, but not identical, to the upperside, but the hindwings underneath have dark markings along the veins and distinct orange tinges in places. With the females there is a gradation in the patterning of different individuals to forms resulting in much more black on the upperside and more black and orange on the lower surfaces. All these forms may sometimes be present together.

The caper white is a very common butterfly and very large migrations often occur even into some areas where the caterpillar food plant does not grow. The eggs are laid on various species of *Capparis*, including the cultivated species, and on the wild *Apophyllum anomalum*, both of which are suitable food plants. Eggs can also be deposited on unsuitable plants, on which the caterpillars cannot feed. A great many eggs can be laid on a single leaf.

The young caterpillars are yellowish with many long hairs. As they develop, the caterpillars become greenish or brownish with lots of raised yellowish spots that bear white hairs. The chrysalids are typical pierid type, attached at the tail end and with a silk girdle around the centre. They vary from white to brown, with various black spots on them.

CHEQUERED SWALLOWTAIL
Papilio demoleus

Group: Papilionids

This swallowtail is brown above, with a very distinct chequered pattern of pale yellow spots all over. It has no tail, however. The underside has a more extensive pattern of yellow spots, and on both the upper and lower side of the hindwing there are a few red spots, with a little blue as well.

▶ **The underside of the chequered swallowtail can be quite different to the upperside.**

▲ **The chequered swallowtail does not have tails to its hindwings.**

They are on the wing in the warmer months and show a tendency to migrate. The eggs are normally laid on various species of *Psoralea*, and sometimes on species of *Citrus* (but they do not always seem able to complete their development on these plants). The young caterpillars are black, developing orange patches as they get older. When mature they are greenish yellow with various orange or yellow spots edged with black, and a pair of short spines at the back and front ends. The chrysalids vary from green to brown.

COMMON BROWN *Heteronympha merope*

Group: Satyrids

The underlying colour of the forewings is brownish orange and in the male has more or less separate dark brown streaks. The female, which is slightly bigger, has a patch of brown on the front wing, with yellow patches on it. It has a rather smaller amount of brown on the hindwings. The undersides of the front wings resemble the uppersides, but the hindwings are mottled dull grey and make the butterflies difficult to spot when resting. Both sexes have an eyespot on the front and hindwings.

In late spring the males appear, but as summer progresses the females increase in number whilst the males decrease. By early autumn there are few males to be seen. It appears that the females probably mate as soon as they emerge from the chrysalids but then have a much longer life and do not begin laying their eggs for several months. Their life span may be increased by a partial resting stage during this long period.

The eggs are laid, or even just dropped, on to various species of grass. The mature caterpillars are very variable in colour, from brown to green, and covered with very short hairs. The chrysalids are formed lying loose among shelter on the ground.

COMMON EGGFLY *Hypolimnas bolina*

Group: Nymphalids

This species varies in number from year to year because it is a more tropical and subtropical species, and the prevailing weather conditions

▲ The male of the common eggfly – a more tropical and subtropical species, but very distinctive.

will no doubt have an impact on the population size, and how far south individuals penetrate. It is such a distinctive butterfly that it merits mention. The males are black on the upperside with a large white spot on each wing. This spot shows a distinct purple edge, or is even completely purple when caught at an angle by the light. The underside is brown with a band of white spots across each wing. It also has further spots around the edges of the wings.

The females are similar to the males on the undersides of the wings but the uppersides are very variable. These can be predominantly brown with a few white markings, to a version that is brown with a distinct row of white spots across the front wing, together with an orange area towards the rear. Sometimes there is a large white spot on the hindwing.

▲ A female of the common eggfly, happy to rest awhile.

◄ **Common eggfly chrysalis.**

In the warmer north the species may be seen at any time but only during the summer further south. The eggs are laid in large batches on the underside of many different plant species, but the most commonly used ones are joyweed (*Alternanthera denticulata*) and Paddy's lucerne (*Sida rhombifolia*). Other plants used include those from the following plant families: Acanthaceae, Portulaceae, Polygonaceae, Rubiaceae and Asteraceae.

The mature caterpillars are dark brown with many dark branched spines and a yellowish line along the sides. They feed mostly at night and may not be so obvious during the day. The chrysalis is quite short and stubby, with numerous short, stout spines along one side, and hangs down from its support by the tail end.

COMMON GRASS BLUE *Zizina labradus*

Group: Lycaenids

This is probably the commonest butterfly in Australia and can be expected in most gardens. The upperside of the male of this small butterfly is a pale bluish colour edged with a thin brown border. The female is similar but has a wider brown border and the blue is of a slightly duller shade. The underside of both is a pale grey with pale brown spotting scattered over it. In the warmer regions it flies all the year but in cooler areas it will not be seen in the colder months.

The eggs are laid on the flower buds and young leaves of many different species in the Papilionaceae family, including the cultivated ones. The small, greenish caterpillars can be pests on cultivated crops. The short, rounded chrysalis is attached to the underside of leaves by the tail end and a silken girdle around the middle. This species is also found in New Zealand.

DOUBLEDAY'S SKIPPER *Toxidia doubledayi*

Group: Hesperiids

The upperside of this skipper is dark brown with a few yellow spots on the front wing, the central one being rather elongated with a bend in the middle. Its underside is slightly lighter with a few yellow spots on the front wing. Adults are on the wing from mid–spring to late autumn. The eggs are laid on grasses. The caterpillars feed at night, sheltering by day inside rolled–up leaves on the ground. They are greenish, paler underneath and have a darker stripe along the back, and tiny blunt spines all over. The chrysalids have a rounded head end and a covering of whitish powder when found inside the leaf shelters used by the caterpillars.

LESSER WANDERER *Danaus chrysippus*

Group: Danaids

This butterfly is also known as the plain tiger, and further details of its life cycle can be found in the section on European butterflies. It can be quite common at times and lays its eggs on introduced species in the genus *Asclepias* (cotton bushes) as well as other plants in the family Asclepiadaceae.

The adults that are found in Australia have an orange background to both the front and hindwings and show less variation than in some other parts of the world.

▲ **The lesser wanderer, or plain tiger.**

MEADOW ARGUS *Junonia villida*

Group: Nymphalids

This butterfly is found throughout most of Australia, and large numbers can be seen migrating from one place to another. It is often seen perched on the ground with its wings spread wide. The upperside is predominantly brown with orange markings and both front and hindwings bear large eyespots that are bordered with orange. The underside of the front wing is marked similarly to the upperside, but is very much paler in background, from buff to almost grey. The underside of the hindwing lacks any obvious eyespot and is also generally pale and mottled with grey and buff.

The eggs are laid singly on a wide range of plant species in several different families. These include the Plantaginaceae (*Plantago* species), Scrophulariaceae (*Antirrhinum* species and *Russelia equisetiformis*), Verbenaceae (*Verbena* species including *V. bonariensis*), Gentianaceae (*Centaurium spicatum*) and several other families. The mature caterpillars are black, with lighter spots generally around the many branched spines that cover the body. The rather squat chrysalids are mottled but essentially dark and hang down by the tail end.

ORCHARD BUTTERFLY *Papilio aegeus*

Group: Papilionids

Although this is a swallowtail it does not have tails to its hindwings. There is a clear distinction between the sexes. The males are black on the upperside with a creamy band of spots across the tip of the front wing and a broad band across the hindwing, with a few red spots towards the end. The underside is similar but lacks the creamy band on the hindwing and has a greater number of red spots.

The female is variable. In the more usual form the front wing has black towards the body and white, crossed with darker veins, towards the outer regions. The hindwing has a broad white patch at the centre and blue and red spots along the outer edge. The underside is similar but has more obvious blue and red spots. Other forms may have more or less white on the wings. Adults

◁ **A male orchard butterfly – one of the swallowtails.**

▷ **A female orchard butterfly.**

▲ **The underside of a male orchard butterfly.**

may fly from mid–spring to late autumn where there are two generations per year, but in warmer parts may be seen all the year round.

As the English name suggests, they are frequently seen in orchards where the females visit to lay eggs on the caterpillar food plant which is normally a cultivated species of citrus (upon which minor damage may occur). They can also be found on *Choisya ternata* in gardens and on many different species in the family Rutaceae outside the gardens.

The young caterpillars resemble bird droppings, being brownish with white patches, but by the time they are mature they are green with some short fleshy spines and various white and brownish stripes, some of which are oblique. The chrysalis is attached by the tail end and is held upright by a silk girdle around the middle. It can vary from green to brown in colour, and is normally attached to a plant stem on, or near, the food plant. The adults emerge in a few weeks, depending on the temperature. Once you have seen this magnificent butterfly feeding on flowers in your garden you will not forget it.

PEA BLUE *Lampides boeticus*

Group: Lycaenids

This is the same butterfly as the long-tailed blue in Europe, where it is considered mainly to be a tropical or subtropical species, although it is often to be found in temperate regions.

In Australia it can be found almost anywhere and is a common butterfly, easily recognized by the tails on the hindwings. Migrations south have been reported in early to mid-spring. It is likely that it is continuously brooded in the warmer regions and can overwinter in some of the cooler areas as chrysalids. The caterpillar food plant includes species of *Crotalaria*, and other plants in the family Papilionaceae, such as peas and beans. Further information is given in the section on European butterflies.

There are many other lycaenid butterflies found in Australia and a few may turn up in gardens in the south-east of the country, but distinguishing between them requires a good local identification book.

PHIGALIA SKIPPER *Trapezites phigalia*

Group: Hesperiids

As with so many other skippers, the uppersides of the wings are predominantly brown with yellow spots on the front, and a larger orange area on the hindwing. The underside is much lighter with a yellow-spotted brown patch on the front wing and around eight rather irregular small brown rings on the hindwing.

Depending on the area they are on the wing from early spring to mid-summer. The eggs are laid singly on the leaves of *Lomandra filiformis*.

The caterpillars feed at night, and during the day they hide among leaf litter at the base of the plants. The older caterpillars are greyish with a pink tinge and have a few indistinct dark lines along the body, and a dark head. The brownish chrysalids are short and thick and are found at the base of the plant or inside leaves that have become dried, and have curled up.

▶ **A wanderer on flowers of *Plumbago auriculata*.**

ROCK RINGLET *Hypocysta euphemia*

Group: Satyrids

This rather small butterfly has predominantly brown wings with numerous thin dark lines crossing them. On the front wing there is a small eyespot near the tip and a larger one further back, and a similar eyespot on the hindwing. The undersides are paler. The overall colour of the female is more orange.

Although not widely distributed it can be seen in some areas of south-east Australia on the walls of houses or rock faces. They fly from early spring to mid-autumn, possibly with two generations per year. The eggs are laid on various grasses and the young caterpillars are at first green whilst older ones are brown with some stripes along the body. The head has a few short spikes on it. The chrysalis is dark and hangs by the tail.

WANDERER *Danaus plexippus*

Group: Danaids

Known in other countries as the monarch or milkweed butterfly, this distinctive species was first recorded in Australia in 1871 and is now likely to be seen in gardens in the east and south-east. It is on the wing all year in the northern areas but only in the warmer months in the south because its caterpillar food plants, which are various species of *Asclepias* (and other plants in the Asclepiadaceae), die down to the ground in colder areas.

Although adults do assemble together in a few places in winter, there do not appear to be any well-defined migration movements in Australia. Further details of this butterfly are given in the sections on New Zealand and North America.

YELLOW ADMIRAL *Vanessa itea*

Group: Nymphalids

Sometimes called the Australian admiral, this is the same species that is found in New Zealand. The front wing is mainly black with an orange–brown base and a broad yellow band across the centre. The hindwing is red-brown shading towards black at the edges. The underside of the front wing is similar, but not identical to the upperside, but the hindwing is dark mottled with paler stripes and spots making the butterfly difficult to spot when perched on bark with closed wings.

They have a preference for sap flows on trees rather than flowers, and are most likely to be seen sunning themselves with open wings during the warmer months. The eggs are laid on plants in the family Urticaceae, such as *Urtica incisa*, *U. urens* and the cultivated *Soleirolia soleirolii*.

The caterpillars feed at night, hiding during the day. When mature they have a broad yellow stripe along the body, which shades from blackish to green and is covered with branched spines. The chrysalids are usually hung up away from the food plant and can even be found on walls and posts.

▲ **The yellow admiral will lay its eggs on the mind-your-own-business plant.**

Did you know?

There is some evidence that the yellow admiral migrates with the Australian painted lady, although the yellow admiral is by no means as widely distributed as that species.

YELLOW-BANDED or SOUTHERN DART *Ocybadistes walkeri*

Group: Hesperiids

The upper surface of this rather small skipper is dark brown with irregular–shaped orange spots. The underside has a distinct greenish tinge to the dark front wing and the yellowish hindwing, both with similar yellow–orange markings to those on the upper surfaces. They are flying from early spring to late autumn, depending on the area.

The eggs are laid on grasses such as couch (*Cynodon dactylon*), kikuyu (*Pennisetum clandestinum*) and *Brachypodium distachyon*. The caterpillars are pale green with darker stripes on the pale head. They hide in shelters made by joining several grass leaves together, and the chrysalids are usually found close to the ground in shelters made from the dry leaf sheaths.

NEW ZEALAND BUTTERFLIES

Of the few species of butterflies that occur in New Zealand, only the following are likely to be seen in gardens.

MONARCH *Danaus plexippus*

Group: Danaids

This is a large and visually striking butterfly with a powerful flight and widespread distribution around the world. It is thought of mainly as a North American species. Because it migrates over vast distances, and overwinters by the million, it is arguably the best-known butterfly in the world. The wings are bright orange–brown with veins picked out in dense black. Although the male and female are similar, the former can be easily distinguished on close inspection by the presence of a short thickened black region on a central vein in the hindwing. The eggs are laid on milkweeds (*Asclepias* species), and the butterfly itself is sometimes called the milkweed butterfly.

▼ **A caterpillar of the monarch or wanderer.**

Planting milkweeds in gardens is one way of encouraging this dramatic butterfly to stay and breed there.

The caterpillar is as handsome as the adult and the chrysalis an equally amazing structure from which the emergence of the adult is one of Nature's truly remarkable events. There are probably several different strains of this butterfly and not all of them are migratory in the true sense of the word, although all are capable of flying long distances. Adults may be seen on the wing from spring through to autumn, especially in the North Island.

AUSTRALIAN PAINTED LADY *Vanessa kershawi*

Group: Nymphalids

This butterfly is generally thought to reach New Zealand by migration from Australia. The numbers seen can vary widely from year to year because it does not appear to be able to overwinter very successfully in New Zealand. Although the caterpillars have been recorded in Australia as feeding on various species of plant, there does not seem to be any extensive breeding in New Zealand. See the section on Australia for more details of this species.

RED ADMIRAL *Vanessa gonerilla*

Group: Nymphalids

Like its European relative and namesake, this species is frequently seen in gardens and is typically attracted to Buddleja in late summer. The background colour of the wings is black with a distinct red bar across the front wing and white blotches above this. The hindwing differs from that of the European red admiral (*Vanessa atalanta*) in having four white–eyed black spots on the red band, which is also somewhat in from the edge of the wing.

The eggs are laid on stinging nettles, where caterpillars can be found from spring to mid–summer. The adults are long–lived and capable of hibernation over the winter, sometimes coming out to fly on warm days.

◁ **The small white is considered a pest on cabbage crops.**

SMALL WHITE *Pieris rapae*

Group: Pierids
This common cabbage white butterfly has been introduced by accident to New Zealand and is considered a pest of cabbages and other brassica crops, although its caterpillars will also feed on other members of the cabbage family, and nasturtiums. The life cycle is short and there are several broods over the warmer months, so the butterfly is a likely visitor to gardens at any time. The species overwinters in the chrysalis stage. There is more information on this species in the section on Europe.

YELLOW ADMIRAL *Vanessa itea*

Group: Nymphalids
This butterfly possesses a yellow band, rather than red, across the front wing. Its caterpillars feed on nettles and the butterfly can be expected to visit gardens, but is more likely to be seen basking in the sun than competing with the red admiral at the buddleja bush. It is a common species also in Australia. The adults are long-lived and capable of overwintering.

The following butterflies may also be seen in New Zealand gardens:

COMMON COPPER *Lycaena salustius*

Group: Lycaenids
The caterpillars feed on plants in the genus *Muehlenbeckia* (Polygonaceae).

DARK-BANDED COPPER
Chrysophanus enysii

Group: Lycaenids
The caterpillars feed on plants in the genus *Muehlenbeckia* (Polygonaceae).

NEW ZEALAND COMMON BLUE
Zizina (= Zizera) *labradus*

Group: Lycaenids
In Australia this is called the common grass blue. See that section for further details.

SMALL COPPER *Lycaena boldenarum*

Group: Lycaenids
The caterpillars feed on plants in the genus *Muehlenbeckia* (Polygonaceae). This is not the same species as the European small copper.

Mainland Europe and the United Kingdom

As might be expected due to its greater size and range of habitats, there are many more butterfly species to be found in mainland Europe than in the United Kingdom. Many of these European species are, however, confined to particular localities and habitats, and when it comes to butterflies that are likely to visit gardens, there are only a few more species for the mainland of Europe as compared to the United Kingdom. The number of individuals of a species seen in Europe may be much larger. In rural areas, where few gardens are scattered amongst large areas of agricultural land, many species other than those mentioned here may visit gardens, and for accurate identification you should consult suitable guides.

BLACK-VEINED WHITE *Aporia crataegi*

Group: Pierids

This butterfly was common in the UK in the early 19th century, but today it is only the very occasional migrant that is ever seen. It is thought that damp winter weather in the UK may have contributed to the extinction of this species there, although many other factors may also have been involved. In Europe the numbers are still large and the

Did you know?

The adults are quite long-lived and can be around for over a month if not caught by birds or spiders. They are particularly fond of purplish flowers such as those of clovers, scabious and knapweeds.

caterpillars may even become a problem in orchards that are not sprayed. The butterfly is a typical pierid ('white') of medium size with only the veins being picked out in black in the male or brown in the female although the latter tend easily to lose the scales from their wings and become almost translucent.

The males can congregate in large numbers at damp mud where they are collecting sodium salts or other minerals that are essential for their fertility. There is only a single brood per year with the adults flying from mid–spring to mid–summer. The caterpillars feed on plants within the family Rosaceae and especially the genus *Prunus*.

The eggs are laid in batches and the caterpillars stay together under a shared web of silk. Long before they are mature, at about only 1/6in (4mm) long, the caterpillars go into hibernation until the following spring. When they wake up the caterpillars feed up, bask in the sun, and only disperse when they grow larger. They pupate during spring (if the weather conditions are suitable) on the food plant, and the adults emerge after a few weeks.

▲ The scales on the wings of the black-veined white are easily lost, making the wings almost translucent.

⚠ **The clouded yellow is a summer migrant to the UK, but common throughout the year in southern Europe.**

BRIMSTONE *Gonepteryx rhamni*

Group: Pierids

The male of the brimstone is brilliant yellow, and the female is a pale greenish–white (it might be mistaken for a large white, although the shape of the wings, with their distinct points, makes the difference clear when the butterflies are at rest, which is always with closed wings).

The adults hibernate and can be seen from early summer when they have emerged from the current season's chrysalids, right through to autumn and again the following year, when they emerge from hibernation in spring.

Pairing is delayed until spring, and the eggs are laid on buckthorn (*Rhamnus cathartica*), alder buckthorn (*R. frangula*) and sometimes other members of the genus. This is usually just when the buds are starting to open and the caterpillar feeds up for about a month before heading for the shorter plants at the base of the shrubby buckthorns in order to pupate. The adults emerge after only a couple of weeks and feed up until autumn when they seek out evergreen shrubs and trees, such as holly and those clothed in ivy, to hibernate. The brimstone occurs in the UK, Europe, North Africa and parts of Asia as far as Japan.

CLOUDED YELLOW *Colias croceus*

Group: Pierids

This butterfly is predominantly bright yellow with black tips to the wings and elsewhere. A small percentage of the females are a pale creamy white instead of bright yellow and might easily be confused with the pale clouded yellow. This is a fast-flying butterfly and rarely perches with its wings open. There are several broods per year and adults may be seen from mid–spring to mid–autumn. Individuals in the south of Europe migrate north each year, but the annual numbers reaching the UK and other northern regions can vary widely. The butterfly cannot overwinter in these cooler climes, regardless of the stage of the life cycle.

Eggs are laid on bird's-foot trefoils, clovers, lucerne and many other plants in the family Papilionaceae. They are laid singly on the upperside of the leaves, and caterpillars take about a month in summer before pupating on the food plant. The last generation each year goes into hibernation in the cooler parts of its range, but may continue to feed in the warmer areas such as the Canary Islands, North Africa and Iran.

◀ **The comma with its characteristic wavy-edged wings.**

COMMA *Polygonia c-album*

Group: Nymphalids

The comma gets its English name from the comma–like white mark that is present on the underside of the dark–brown mottled hindwings. The uppersides of the wings are an orange–brown or yellow with numerous dark spots, but the most characteristic feature is the very jagged outer margins to the wings.

The adult butterfly emerges from its hibernation in spring, and two generations per year are produced. The first is on the wing in early summer and the second from early autumn till they settle down for hibernation in some dark sheltered place. They can often be seen in gardens feeding at buddleja and other flowers, and will suck the juice from overripe fruit. The butterfly is present in the UK and Europe, except for the more northern regions, in North Africa and parts of Asia as far as Japan.

The eggs are laid singly, or a few together, on the edge of the leaves of several different plants including hops, stinging nettles, elms, sallows and even currants (genus *Ribes*). The caterpillars may feed up very quickly, pupate and produce adults in mid–summer (which are rather paler than their parents), or they will feed slowly and then pupate to form adults of the darker shade in late summer. During this slow feeding the other, paler adults have bred and produced another generation of adults, which are also of the darker form so that all the butterflies that hibernate are of the darker form.

The caterpillars of both forms are similar, and when fully grown are quite distinctive, having a large white area at the hind end while the rest of the body is mainly brown, with branched spines being present all over the body. It is thought that this white patch makes the caterpillar look rather like a bird–dropping and so helps to prevent it from being eaten by birds. The chrysalis is formed on the food plant or close by.

Separate species of comma

The American comma is very similar but considered a separate species, *Polygonia comma*. The southern comma found in south-east Europe, which has rather fewer spots on the upperside, is also considered a separate species, *Polygonia egea*.

GATEKEEPER *Pyronia tithonus*

Group: Satyrids

The uppersides of the wings are predominantly orange with broad brown borders. Double black spots with white central eyes, visible on both upper and lower sides of the wings, are situated towards the tip of the front wings. The male is easily distinguished from the female because he has a broad brown sex brand across the centre of the front wing. The butterfly is found in the southern half of the UK and central and southern Europe.

It is on the wing from mid–summer to mid–autumn. This late appearance is due to the fact that the overwintering stage is the young caterpillar, which then feeds up in spring. The eggs are laid on, or even just scattered over, the food plants, which are various species of grass. The mature caterpillar is greenish or brownish with lighter stripes along the side and it pupates low down on the grasses. Although like most satyrids this is a butterfly of grassy fields, it is one of the few that fairly regularly visit gardens.

▼ **A gatekeeper struggling to find nectar in a double *Coreopsis grandiflora* 'Mayfield Giant'.**

▲ **The geranium bronze is considered a pest in some places because its caterpillars eat pelargoniums.**

GERANIUM BRONZE *Cacyreus marshalli*

Group: Lycaenids

This is a butterfly that has its main base in South Africa but which has spread to southern Europe and is likely to turn up further north wherever there is a strong trade in plants, because its main caterpillar food plant is the pelargonium. It is a small butterfly with a brown upperside and a chequered margin, with a lighter and patterned underside. The flight is weak and mostly near to the ground and, depending on the climate, it may be seen from late spring to mid–autumn (although in very warm climates it could breed all the year round).

The eggs are laid on the flowers and the caterpillars feed on the developing seeds. It can become a pest where pelargoniums are grown on a large scale. It can also live on various species in the genus *Geranium* and so has the potential to become established, in warmer areas, on native rather than cultivated plants. No true butterfly lover would begrudge the loss of a few flower blooms in exchange for this charming invader, but commercial growers might have a different point of view.

GREEN-VEINED WHITE *Pieris napi*

Group: Pierids

This butterfly is about the same size as the small white but, at least in the early season broods, is easily distinguished from it when at rest with closed wings, due to the heavy dark markings along the veins of the underside of the hindwings. It is not a pest as it does not lay eggs on cultivated brassicas, and it rarely breeds in gardens. In the wild the green caterpillars feed singly on charlock (*Sinapis arvensis*), garlic mustard (*Alliaria petiolata*), cuckoo flower (*Cardamine pratensis*) and watercress (*Nasturtium officinale*), but in the garden may take lavender or buddleja leaves.

The adults are on the wing from early spring to late autumn and there may be one or up to four broods per year depending on the conditions. To some extent the butterflies' genetic make-up will influence the number of generations as some northern strains appear only ever to produce one per year. In other cases chrysalids may remain in the resting state for a whole year, whereas others in the same batch emerge after only a few weeks to give a second brood.

The butterfly is found in the UK, Europe, North Africa, parts of Asia and in North America, but there is never much sign of mass migrations as with the other common white butterflies. There are probably several subspecies of this butterfly, which show differences in wing colouration and markings as well as the details of the timing of the life cycles.

HOLLY BLUE *Celastrina argiolus*

Group: Lycaenids

The name 'holly blue' refers to the main food plant used by the first-brood caterpillars of this double-brooded butterfly. A wide range of other plants may also be used by this first generation, provided they are in flower at the time of egg-laying, because the eggs are laid on the flowers and they feed on them and the developing fruits. Other plants used include bell heather, blackberry, dogwood, gorse, hop, raspberry and spindle. The second brood mostly feed on ivy flowers and fruit.

Both the male and female of this small butterfly have blue on the upperside of the wings, but in the male this is more violet-blue and with a thinner black margin to the wings. It is on the wing from mid-spring to early autumn and obtains its food from flowers and oozing sap, as well as honeydew on leaves deposited by aphids and other pests. The holly blue often flies high up in the tops of shrubs and trees.

It is found in most parts of the UK and Europe except the colder regions, and in North Africa and Asia as far as Japan. The caterpillars are short and dumpy, greenish at first but becoming reddish as they mature, and are often attended on the food plant by ants. The first brood may pupate on the leaves but the second brood usually finds a more protective crevice because this is the overwintering stage of the life cycle.

LARGE WHITE/CABBAGE WHITE
Pieris brassicae

Group: Pierids

This is common in both the UK and Europe and extends into Asia and North Africa. It is a migratory species and the population existing in the cooler parts of its range, such as the UK, is often supplemented by large numbers from warmer parts. While migrating, the flight is more powerful and directed than when casually flying in gardens.

▲ **The greenish-yellow caterpillars of the large white.**

▲ **A female large white, also called the cabbage white. The amount of black seen can vary with the time of year.**

A typical 'white' butterfly, the males have rather less black markings than the females, but the amount of black on both sexes can vary with the time of year. There can be up to three broods and the later ones tend to have more black on them.

They can be on the wing from mid–spring to mid–autumn and they should not be denigrated just because they are common and may be troublesome in the kitchen garden. The batches of bright yellow eggs are familiar on cultivated cabbages and other brassica crops, but in the wild are laid on several different members of the brassica family. The caterpillars are greenish–yellow, mottled with black, and stay close together for most of their life, only separating when fully grown to find a pupation spot, which can be some distance from the food plant. Apart from the cabbages and their close relatives, the caterpillars may also feed on nasturtiums and crambe in the garden, and wild mignonette elsewhere. The last brood of chrysalids overwinter, apparently in response to shortening day lengths, and emerge the following spring.

Did you know?

The numbers of the large white are strongly controlled by the tiny parasitoid wasp, *Apanteles glomeratus*. However, this is only of subsequent help to the vegetable gardener because the caterpillars have already done their damage before they die surrounded by the wasps' yellow silk cocoons. The majority of caterpillars collected from plants outdoors are often already doomed, even when quite small.

LONG-TAILED BLUE *Lampides boeticus*

Group: Lycaenids

This butterfly is very common in subtropical and tropical regions of the Old World and is resident all the year in southern Europe and North Africa, from where it annually migrates northwards. Only rarely does it reach the UK. As the name suggests, it has an obvious tail to the hindwing.

As with many species of blue butterfly it is the male upperside that is mostly blue with only a thin black border, while that of the female is mostly dark brown with only a small central patch of blue. The adults may be seen for a long period from mid–spring to mid–autumn, as a result of two or three broods produced in the year, depending on the climate.

The eggs are laid singly on the flowers of plants in the family Papilionaceae – including cultivated broad beans and peas, as well as wild plants such as gorse (*Ulex europaeus*), everlasting peas (*Lathyrus* species), lupin (*Lupinus nootkatensis*), senna (*Senna* species) and others. After eating the flowers the caterpillars move into the developing seedpods, which they eat before reaching full size and then leaving.

They pupate on the ground amongst stones and leaves. This is the overwintering stage in colder parts of its resident range, but in the warmer regions it can be brooded continuously, and can then reach pest status on host crops.

MAP BUTTERFLY *Araschnia levana*

Group: Nymphalids

The English name of this butterfly refers to the fine white lines found on the underside of the wings, the background of which is brownish–purple. There are two broods per year and they are very different in colour from each other. The first adults have a rich orange background to the upper surface of the wings with many dark spots and a few white ones near the tips of the front wings.

The second–brood adults have a dark brown background and a broad creamy–white band running right across the centre of the wings and an orange band of fine dashes around the outer edge of the hindwings, sometimes extending into the front wings. The difference between the appearance of the adults of the two broods has been related to the different lengths of daylight hours during their development as caterpillars. The first adults, emerging from the overwintering chrysalids, are on the wing in mid–spring and some adults of the second generation may take the flight period through until mid–autumn.

The eggs are laid on stinging nettle and are unusual in that they are laid in a chain that extends out from the leaf surface, often made up of a dozen or more eggs. The caterpillars are black, with dark branched spines over the body and a couple of distinct spikes on the head. The caterpillars usually stay fairly close together when feeding. The chrysalids are generally formed on the food plant. The map butterfly is found in central parts of Europe, but not in the UK, and across parts of Asia to Japan. At one time it was introduced into the UK and established itself in part of the Forest of Dean, but it was deliberately destroyed there and no longer occurs on the UK list. It does seem to be extending its range naturally and may colonize the UK in the future.

MONARCH *Danaus plexippus*

Group: Danaids

This butterfly, which is thought of mainly for its long–distance migrations in America, has established itself in parts of southern Europe and has long been bred by butterfly enthusiasts

▷ **A monarch on flowers of *Asclepias curassavica*.**

in their greenhouses. One of its caterpillar food plants, the blood flower (*Asclepias curassavica*), is grown extensively in gardens as a summer herbaceous plant, which is not frost hardy but can be overwintered in a frost–free greenhouse (other species in the genus have underground storage organs that allow them to overwinter). The monarch is listed as a UK species as well as European, and is established in the Canary Islands and the Azores.

The eggs are laid singly on milkweed, and the caterpillars are boldly marked with yellow and black rings and have a pair of black filaments at each end. The rather short and stubby chrysalis hangs down from its supporting stem or leaf and is generally a jade green with distinct gold markings around it. The butterfly cannot overwinter in cold climates and most of those seen in the cooler parts of their range have come from warmer climes. The monarch is also mentioned in the Australian and New Zealand sections of this chapter.

NETTLE-TREE BUTTERFLY *Libythea celtis*

Group: Nymphalids

This medium–sized butterfly is only found in the southern parts of Europe, North Africa and across parts of Asia to Japan. The upperside is predominantly dark brown, with large orange irregular spots. When resting, with wings closed, the underside of the hindwing is dull brown with a white streak in the centre that can, coupled with the rather irregular shape of the wings, suggest that it might be a comma.

There is normally only one generation per year, although a quick spring brood is possible in some places. Adults may be flying from early summer to early autumn and then go into hibernation until early spring, generally hiding in dense shrubby vegetation. Small groups of eggs are laid in spring on the young leaves of the nettle tree (*Celtis australis*), which is sometimes also called the hackberry. The caterpillars are green or brown with a lighter stripe along the side. This butterfly generally pupates on the lower surface of the leaves of the food plant and the adults emerge within a couple of weeks. The adults are often seen at blackberry flowers and even at the ripe fruits, as well as at the flowers of Christ's thorn (*Paliurus spina-christi*).

ORANGE TIP *Anthocharis cardamines*

Group: Pierids
The upper surface of the female orange tip's wings resemble those of the small white, but when at rest with its wings closed the mottled green underside of the hindwing makes it clearly different – even if it is then difficult to find.

This is because it is only the male that has the orange tips to its wings. The butterflies are flying from early spring to mid–summer and an occasional adult may be seen in late summer.

It is not certain whether this is a genuine second brood or merely late emergence, because the butterfly is normally single–brooded and spends both autumn and winter as a chrysalis.

The orange tip is found in the UK, Europe and parts of Asia. The caterpillars feed on cuckoo flower, garlic mustard, hedge mustard (*Sisymbrium officinale*) and occasionally on watercress. In gardens they can often be found on honesty (*Lunaria annua*) and sweet rocket (*Hesperis matronalis*).

The eggs are laid on the flowering parts of the plants, singly, and are at first white but soon turn orange. The caterpillars are often difficult to spot amongst the flowers and developing seedpods; they occur singly because if they meet another of their kind one will eat the other. The chrysalis is formed on the food plant and tends to be a very thin and angular structure, resembling a thorn on the stem.

▲ A female orange tip feeding at flowers of *Leptospermum scoparium*.

▲ Only the male orange tip has orange tips to its wings.

▲ **The painted lady is one of the most widely distributed butterflies in the world.**

PAINTED LADY *Vanessa cardui*

Group: Nymphalids

This familiar UK and European butterfly is, in fact, one of the most widely distributed species and is found all over the world where the climate is not too cold, except for South America.

The upper surface of the wing is mottled with black and white patches over an orange-red background and there is a profusion of orange-brown hairs by the body. In temperate regions the butterfly may be seen from mid-spring to mid-autumn, but in the warmer climates it flies all year round. It does not, however, survive the whole year in many places where the winter temperatures are too low, and that includes the UK and almost all of Europe. Its presence in summer in such places is due to its very strong flight and migratory tendency, which allows huge numbers to travel northwards from North Africa where it breeds the whole year round.

The painted lady has a very long list of possible caterpillar food plants. There may be different strains that prefer particular plants, or groups of plants, but there seems to be great flexibility. Thistles may be used, and these are common and invasive plants. In other places stinging nettles, mallows (*Malva species*) and even some crops may be used. The eggs are laid singly on the upperside of the leaves and the young caterpillar moves underneath and spins a thin covering of silk under which it eats away the lower surface of the leaf. Mature caterpillars make larger tents of silk and leaf, hiding their mottled black and yellowish bodies and prominent spines. The chrysalis is usually formed on the food plant under the leaves and is pinkish grey with some golden yellow spots. There is no resting or hibernation stage in the life cycle, and the adults emerge within a couple of weeks.

PEACOCK *Inachis io*

Group: Nymphalids

This butterfly is quite distinctive with its bright eyespots on the upperside of both front and hindwings, which themselves have a maroon-brown background with darker margins. The underside is very dark and makes the butterfly difficult to see when it is hibernating – which it does as the adult. Eggs are laid in spring, after hibernation, and are piled in large groups on the underside of stinging-nettle leaves.

The caterpillars are black and spiny, with a scattering of fine white spots on the body. They remain together amongst a few threads of silk until fully grown when they wander off to pupate, often some distance from the food plant. The adults emerge after a couple of weeks and live for a long time, often being seen feeding at buddleja, before hibernation. The species is very mobile and moves readily from place to place and is common in the UK and Europe, apart from the very coldest regions.

▲ **A caterpillar of the peacock butterfly.**

Except in the warmest parts of its range there is usually only one generation per year, but because of its long life span it is possible to see last year's adults while the present year's are also flying.

PLAIN TIGER *Danaus chrysippus*

Group: Danaids

This butterfly is only likely to be seen in the most southern parts of Europe where it is a summer visitor from Africa. It breeds on milkweed, which can be widespread due to the light feathery seeds that can be carried long distances by wind. The plain tiger could possibly survive winter in some warmer places, but its presence is mostly due to new arrivals each spring.

In Africa there are several colour forms of this butterfly, but the usual one to be found in Europe has an orange or reddish upperside to the wings, with the front ones tipped black overlaid with white spots. The hindwings have a black margin. The male has a distinct additional black spot on the centre of the hindwing, referred to as a sex brand.

The eggs are laid singly on the leaves of milkweed (*Asclepias* species), and are distinctively patterned with black and yellow banding. Along the length of the caterpillar there are three pairs of black filaments. The chrysalis is short and fat, hangs down from its support, and is green or pale pinkish–brown embellished with a few golden yellow spots. Although it has a very rapid life cycle in Africa, producing many broods per year, it is likely to have only one or two in southern Europe.

▼ **A caterpillar of the plain tiger on a half-eaten milkweed seedpod. Note the three pairs of black filaments.**

▲ **A male plain tiger, with wings closed.**

QUEEN OF SPAIN FRITILLARY
Issoria lathonia

Group: Nymphalids

Like many other fritillaries this butterfly has an orange–brown upper surface to the wings with many dark spots all over it. The main distinguishing feature is on the lower side of the hindwing, which has many large, shiny, silvery spots on a brownish background. The butterfly is found throughout Europe, except the far north, but it is only seen in the UK as a very occasional visitor. It is also found in North Africa and across parts of Asia to China.

The reason for its absence from the UK is not clear, because the caterpillar food plant (species of *Viola*, especially pansies) is plentiful there. It migrates extensively in Europe and may be on the wing from late winter to mid-autumn, there being two or more generations per year. The winter can be passed as an adult, a chrysalis or a caterpillar, and it may be that none of these stages is sufficiently robust to survive a winter in the UK.

The eggs are laid singly and the caterpillars are mainly black with some white and brown markings and reddish–brown branched spines. The chrysalis is formed close to the ground and has been described as looking rather like a bird–dropping. The adults normally emerge within a couple of weeks if conditions are suitable.

RED ADMIRAL *Vanessa atalanta*

Group: Nymphalids

This well–known butterfly, with its red stripe across the black of the front wings, plus a few white spots, and the red edge to the hindwings, is a familiar visitor to gardens throughout the UK and Europe. It can be on the wing from late spring to mid–autumn and in the warmer southern parts of its range again in the early spring after hibernation. Only a few individuals seem to overwinter in the UK and other northern parts of its range, where there is only one generation per year. Note that this is a different species to the red admiral found in New Zealand.

The red admiral is highly mobile and migrates each year to repopulate the northern regions; it shows some inclination to return southwards at the end of the year. In the warmer parts of its range there may be two generations per year. The normal food plant is the stinging nettle, but occasionally hop may be used. The eggs are laid singly or in pairs on the upper surface of the leaves and the young caterpillar draws the edges of the leaf together to form a tent. As it grows this is repeated and the caterpillar becomes darkish, with white and yellowish spots and many sturdy spines. The chrysalis is often hidden inside the last leaf used by the caterpillar, and the adults emerge after a few weeks. The adults are noted for their fondness for rotting fruit in autumn, as well as their frequent visits to buddleja flowers.

▲ A red admiral, mainly a European summer visitor to the UK.

▲ A red admiral feeding at buddleja flowers.

Did you know?

There is evidence that some red admirals may be able to overwinter in sheltered places in the UK, and certainly enthusiasts have been able to keep them alive over the winter with a little care and attention.

SCARCE SWALLOWTAIL *Iphiclides podalirius*

Group: Papilionids

As far as Europe is concerned this is quite a common butterfly. The epithet 'scarce' refers to the fact that it is very rarely seen in the United Kingdom except for the odd specimen that has somehow managed to make the journey, or has escaped from a private breeding programme. This is an obvious large swallowtail and the forewing has six black stripes on a pale yellow to almost white background. The hindwing has a black border and distinct blue markings along its outer edge.

The adults can be seen from early spring to early summer and mid–summer to early autumn in southern Europe, where there are two broods per year. In the northern regions, and at higher altitudes, there is only one brood, which is seen on the wing from mid–spring to mid–summer. When the butterfly is at rest, with its wings closed, the underside at the 'tail' end of the wings may give birds the impression that it is the head end. This will, therefore, help it to escape fatal predation.

The caterpillars feed on many species in the family Rosaceae, such as blackthorn (*Prunus spinosa*), which is also known as sloe, as well as cultivated plums and cherries; they may therefore be expected in orchards, hedgerows and open woodland as well as gardens. The caterpillars usually pupate on the food plant and can be found at most times of the year. The overwintering stage is the chrysalis. This tends to be brown when overwintering but green during summer months when the leaves are on the food plant.

SMALL COPPER *Lycaena phlaeas*

Group: Lycaenids

As its name suggests this butterfly is both small and has a distinct coppery colour on the upperside of the forewing, although this is offset by a dark marginal band and several dark spots. Depending on the climate there can be up to four generations per year and the butterfly might be seen from late winter to late autumn in some parts of its range. This extends from the UK through Europe to Asia and Japan, North Africa and even North America where it is known as the American copper. The butterfly has a fast, darting flight and the males, despite their small size, are quite prepared to defend their favourite patch of vegetation from others.

The usual caterpillar food plants are sorrels and docks in the genus *Rumex*, and they can often be detected at a young age because they eat away the lower surfaces of the leaves to make obvious 'windows' rather than holes in the leaves. Although they can pupate quite quickly in warm weather, the last generation each year passes the winter as a caterpillar, feeding up on warm days but otherwise hiding away at the base of the plant. The rather short, fat and rounded chrysalis can be on the plant itself or down in the leaf litter at its base. Note that the butterfly called small copper in Australia is a totally different species.

▲ **A small copper caught with wings fully open.**

▲ **A small copper in typical resting pose.**

SMALL SKIPPER *Thymelicus sylvestris*

Group: Hesperiids

This is one of the few members of its group that is likely to find its way into gardens. As the name suggests, it is a small butterfly and it has golden orange wings with a darker margin. The male has a dark streak, a sex brand, across the centre of the front wing. The rather narrow triangular front wings and the habit of raising these front wings at an angle to the hindwings when basking in the sun make it fairly easy to recognize. Although there is only one generation per year, the adults emerge over many months and can be seen from early spring until late summer.

The butterfly is found in the UK and most of Europe except the far north and also in North Africa and the nearer parts of Asia. The eggs are laid a few together in the bases of grass leaves where the caterpillars emerge but rapidly spin a silk cover and go into winter hibernation, waking again in spring to continue feeding inside a silk–bound tube of grass leaves. It pupates wrapped loosely in grass leaves, emerging as an adult only when ready.

▲ **A small skipper on thistle flowers with wings held at the normal angles.**

SMALL TORTOISESHELL *Aglais urticae*

Group: Nymphalids

This familiar garden butterfly is present in the UK, Europe and temperate parts of Asia and may be the same as, or is very similar to, the North American *Aglais milberti*. The main colour on the upperside of the wings is orange–yellow with a thin border of blue-spotted black, except for the front of the forewings where there are three large black spots. A few more dark spots and a mass of orange–brown hairs alongside the body complete the most attractive upperside of this butterfly. The underside of the hindwings is dark with a wavy– edged lighter tinge towards the outer edge, making the butterfly particularly difficult to spot in dark places during winter hibernation.

The small tortoiseshell is highly mobile and active, and in many years is one of the commonest garden butterflies. It emerges from hibernation in early spring and there are then two or three generations, with the first brood generally appearing in early summer. Depending on the climate the butterfly usually goes into hibernation in mid–autumn. The main caterpillar food plant is the perennial stinging nettle (*Urtica dioica*), but other nettles and even hop have been used. The eggs are laid in large masses on the underside of the leaves. The caterpillars live in a mass in silk nests on the food plant until they disperse when fully grown, at which time they are mainly black, speckled with yellowish white and with yellow bands along the side, together with dark branched spines all over. The chrysalis forms on the food plant or nearby, and the adults emerge within a few weeks.

SMALL WHITE/CABBAGE WHITE
Pieris rapae

Group: Pierids

As the name suggests, this butterfly is smaller than the large white. It does, however, have a similar appearance, except that the dark markings on the wings are grey rather than black and there is some difference in the position and extent of the markings. There are two or more broods per year depending on the conditions. The later broods have darker markings and towards the end of the season the size of the butterflies tends to decrease.

This is one of the commonest butterflies in the world, being found in the UK, Europe, Asia and introduced into North America, Australia and New Zealand. Wherever cabbages are grown it can be a significant pest, but it is still an attractive butterfly when considered for itself. Despite its small size it is a strong migrant, moving to cooler climes in spring and early summer, and to warmer places towards autumn. The caterpillars feed on cultivated brassicas, nasturtiums, crambe and in the wild on many species in the brassica family, and mignonette. The eggs are laid singly and the caterpillars feed separately, being mainly green and rather difficult to see, especially as they may get deep inside leaves that are curled round one another. The autumn chrysalis is the overwintering stage, and it is usually formed away from the food plant. Due to its feeding habits as a caterpillar it is less subject to attack by parasitoid wasps than the large white.

▲ **A small tortoiseshell with wings outstretched.**

North America

North America is very large and has a huge climatic range. In this book we can focus only on a few of the common butterflies likely to visit gardens in the parts of the USA that can be considered to have an essentially temperate climate. Even here, however, with the absence of significant barriers to northward migration, it follows that many butterflies preferring warmer climates have the opportunity to move northwards as temperatures rise, perhaps during the course of several generations. These butterflies may not be able to overwinter in the northern regions, but will be replaced by fresh individuals each year. A rather similar situation exists for a few of the species found in the UK and Europe.

AMERICAN COPPER *Lycaena phlaeas*

Group: Lycaenids

Sometimes called the small copper, this butterfly is the same species as is found in Europe and the UK. It is on the wing from spring to autumn in the north–eastern states, and in various places in the western mountains. The butterfly is described in the section on European and UK butterflies, and the caterpillars feed on the same species of sorrel (*Rumex acetosella*) and curled dock (*Rumex crispus*) as in the UK, from where both of these plants have been introduced and are now common weeds. In the western mountains the food plant is usually mountain sorrel (*Oxyria digyna*).

▲ **American copper or small copper – the name depends on where you live.**

AMERICAN PAINTED LADY
Vanessa virginiensis

Group: Nymphalids

Although numbers can vary widely from year to year, this butterfly occurs throughout the USA. The upper surface of the wings is similar to that of the painted lady although the basic colour may be a little more yellow–orange. There are black tips to the wings with white spots on them, and other black spots of various sizes on the wings, some forming a border around the wings above which, on the hindwings, are some blue spots. The underside is strongly patterned with two large eyespots on the hindwings.

There are two to four broods every year, depending on the region, and both adults and chrysalids are able to overwinter. The eggs are laid on a number of different plants in the family Asteraceae, especially *Anaphalis margaritacea* and *Gnaphalium obtusifolium*. The caterpillars are mostly black with yellow bands and white spots along the sides.

ANISE SWALLOWTAIL *Papilio zelicaon*

Group: Papilionids

This butterfly is black on the upperside with a band of yellow spots across the centre of both the front and hindwings. There are also some patches of blue on the hindwings, together with an orange eyespot at the tail end of the inner margin. Wild anise – or more accurately, fennel, and not the true anise (*Pimpinella anisum*) – is the caterpillar food plant. Fennel is often grown in gardens as a herb, and this will bring the anise swallowtail into them.

It is found in the western parts of the USA and is on the wing in early and mid–summer in the more northern parts of its range, but may be seen all the year round in the warmer southern parts. Eggs are also laid on carrot, parsley and other members of the family Apiaceae, and sometimes on citrus. Like many other swallowtails the young caterpillars look like bird–droppings while the older ones are green with black bands and some yellow spots. Where it has a resting stage over the winter this is as a chrysalis.

BLACK SWALLOWTAIL *Papilio polyxenes*

Group: Papilionids

This butterfly is considered to be a mimic of the pipevine swallowtail and as the name suggests is mainly black on the upper surface of the wings. This is brightened by rows of yellow spots along the margins of the front wings, and the hindwings have additional blue patches and a couple of orange and black eyespots near the inner tail margin. It is mostly seen from spring to autumn, but the season may be extended somewhat in the warmer parts of the USA. The eggs are laid on carrot, celery and parsley in the family Apiaceae.

The young caterpillars look like bird–droppings but the older ones are green with a few black stripes, ornamented with yellowish spots. It overwinters as a chrysalis. Because it is less common in the western parts of the USA this butterfly is sometimes called the eastern black swallowtail.

BUCKEYE *Junonia coenia*

Group: Nymphalids

The Latin name of this species is sometimes given as *Precis coenia*. Its English name refers to the large eyespots on the front and hindwings, which stand out clearly on an orangey–brown, somewhat patterned, background.

It is mainly a year–round resident of the south, but migrations each year take it to most of the north with the exception of the north–west. The eggs are laid on a wide range of plants including weedy plantains *Plantago* species), toadflax *Linaria* species), snapdragons (*Antirrhinum*), and many other wild and garden plants. The caterpillars are dark with spines all down the body. Depending on the climate there can be two to four generations per year but there is little indication that it can overwinter in the north. The adults have a habit of sunning themselves on bare ground, taking off with a very rapid flight if disturbed.

CHECKERED SKIPPER *Pyrgus communis*

Group: Hesperiids

This skipper has a distinct pattern of white and brownish–black areas on the upperside of its wings. It may visit gardens all over the USA and will be on the wing all the year in the south and from spring to autumn in the north. Like most skippers, the adults take frequent, but short, fast flights. There may be several generations per year, depending on the local climate.

The eggs are laid on various plants in the family Malvaceae, including hollyhocks *Alcea rosea*, formerly *Althaea rosea*) and mallows (*Malva* species), as well as plants in other genera. The caterpillars can be greenish yellow to near brown, with short white hairs on the body, and a dark head. They can overwinter either as well–grown caterpillars, or as chrysalids where the winters are cold.

▲ *Junonia almana* **is a butterfly from south-east Asia, and is very similar to the buckeye of America.**

The arctic skipper

The checkered skipper is an entirely different species to the European chequered skipper (*Carterocephalus palaemon*), which has declined in numbers in the UK. The European form of skipper occurs in the USA, where it is called the arctic skipper. Despite its name it does not live in the Arctic, but in the forests and meadows of northern states and Canada.

CHECKERED WHITE *Pontia (= Pieris) protodice*

Group: Pierids

Although this butterfly is mainly white it has a few dark spots on the front wing, which give it its English name. It can be seen in almost all of the USA from spring to autumn in the northern parts, and all year round in the south. With members of the brassica family, such as cabbage, mustard and turnip as the caterpillar food plants, it is frequently seen in gardens. It also uses the spider or bee plant (*Cleome spinosa*) for egg-laying. The caterpillars are green with yellow and greyish striping, and the final brood of the year overwinters as chrysalids.

CLOUDED SULPHUR *Colias philodice*

Group: Pierids

This is sometimes known as the mud puddle butterfly because the males often congregate at damp mud (although this is a habit shown by the males of many species as they take up mineral salts which are necessary for a successful reproductive capability). Also known as the common sulphur, this butterfly is present in most of the USA except for some parts in the very far south. The upperside of the wings are yellow with a dark band around the edge and a black spot on each front wing. Although considered a pest by many farmers because it uses clovers, alfalfa and some other members of the pea family as caterpillar food plants, it can also be attracted to gardens containing some of these plants. It is seen most often from spring to autumn, but is around for rather longer in the warmer regions. The caterpillars are a darkish green with some darker and lighter stripes along the length of the body. The last generation each year overwinters as chrysalids.

CLOUDLESS SULPHUR *Phoebis sennae*

Group: Pierids

Sometimes known as the cloudless giant sulphur, the females may be of any shade from white through yellow to almost orange, although the males are uniformly yellow. This butterfly is absent from the north-west regions of the USA, but is common all year round in the south. During warmer weather it migrates northwards but it cannot survive the cold winters there and often moves back towards warmer climates at the end of the season. The eggs are laid on various species in the genus *Cassia*, and the caterpillars are greenish with some darker bands across the body. There is no hibernation stage and the northern populations must be renewed each year by fresh arrivals from the south.

FIERY SKIPPER *Hylephila phyleus*

Group: Hesperiids

From its base in the south, where it flies all the year round, this butterfly migrates to some, but not all, of the northern USA each spring, and can there be on the wing until autumn. It does not overwinter in these colder regions. The predominant colour of the male's wings is orange-yellow with a number of darker spots and streaks; the female is altogether darker. In the south there may be as many as five generations each year, with fewer to the north. The eggs are laid on various species of grass, such as bents (*Agrostis* species), Bermuda grass (*Cynodon dactylon*) and even sugar cane (*Saccharum officinarum*). The caterpillars are dark green with small black hairs along the body, and a dark head. In the garden they are largely able to escape the dangers of the mower because they shelter down at the base of the grasses.

GIANT SWALLOWTAIL *Papilio cresphontes*

Group: Papilionids

This is found in most of the USA except the north-west, and like many other species is most common in the warmer south where it can be seen all the year round. Further north it is on the wing from spring to autumn. The upper surface of its wings is black, with a very extensive pattern of yellow spots together with some blue spots near to the tail end of the hindwings.

▲ **A freshly emerged giant swallowtail drying its wings.**

The eggs are laid on various species in the genus *Citrus*, and can be so numerous as to be considered a pest (when they are referred to as 'orange dogs'). They will also feed on various other species in the rue plant family (Rutaceae). The caterpillars are brownish with a mottled pattern of white, and where hibernation occurs it is as the chrysalis.

GRAY HAIRSTREAK *Strymon melinus*

Group: Lycaenids

As its name suggests this small butterfly is grey with the upperside darker than the lower, and there are a couple of orange spots close to the tails on the hindwings. It occurs all over the USA and is on the wing in the north from late spring to mid–autumn, and both earlier and later in the south. The hibernation stage is the chrysalis. The eggs are laid on a wide range of plants including hibiscus, clover, cotton and many others. When its numbers grow too large it can be considered a pest on bean and cotton crops. The caterpillars can be from green to brown, and even reddish.

GREAT SPANGLED FRITILLARY
Speyeria cybele

Group: Nymphalids

This is one of the larger fritillaries, with prominent silvery spots on the lower surface of the wings and the typical orange-brown upper surface, patterned with numerous dark lines and spots. It is found in most of the USA except the southernmost parts, and is on the wing from mid–summer to early autumn, there being only one generation per year. The eggs are laid on various species of violets and, soon after hatching, the caterpillars settle down to hibernate over the winter and then feed up in the spring before pupating.

▲ **The clearly visible silvery spots of the underside of the gulf fritillary.**

▲ A gulf fritillary on an inflorescence of *Buddleja x weyeriana*.

GULF FRITILLARY *Agraulis vanillae*

Group: Heliconids

Although the heliconids are predominantly tropical butterflies, this is one of the few that each summer spreads out through the southern half of the USA from a permanent place in California and warmer places further south. They often move in quite large numbers together.

The upperside of the wings is orange–brown with fine black lines along the veins which broaden out towards the edges, with numerous black spots, some having white eyes to them. The undersides have many silvery spots on a brownish background.

The caterpillars are rather mottled in appearance with black spines over reddish stripes on a dark brown to black body. The caterpillar food plants are passion flowers (*Passiflora* species) and these are commonly seen growing in gardens.

The chrysalis hangs from its tail end from stems, or under leaves, and the adults emerge quite quickly so that there are many broods in the warmer regions. There is no capability for the species to overwinter in frosty places.

▶ A monarch on a flower of *Aeschynanthus javanicus*. Mass migrations of this butterfly are well known.

MONARCH *Danaus plexippus*

Group: Danaids

Although this large and powerful butterfly has been mentioned in other sections, its home is primarily America. The rich orange–brown wings are edged with black borders, spotted with white, and the black veins stand out clearly. The male has a dark sex brand on the hindwing that shows as a dark spot along one of the veins. In the north it is seen from spring to autumn, and in the south all the year round.

The mass migrations to overwinter in Mexico and California are well known, and this butterfly has been the subject of much adulation. The adults are unpalatable to most birds due to substances taken up from the food plants of the caterpillars. These are mostly species in the genus *Asclepias* although other species in the family Asclepiadaceae are also used.

The caterpillars are also boldly marked with yellow, black and white stripes, which advertises their unpleasant taste. There are usually two or more generations in the north and many in the south because there is no resting stage in the life cycle (apart from the adults overwintering), and growth of the caterpillar is very rapid.

Those adults that reach the north may not be the same generation as those that overwintered further south. Extreme adverse weather conditions can kill very many of the overwintering adults, as this is not a rigid hibernation state and if there are warm days the adults may take flight for a few hours before returning to their communal roosts.

PAINTED LADY *Vanessa cardui*

Group: Nymphalids
This butterfly has already been described in the sections on Europe and Australia. It is sometimes called the 'cosmopolitan' because it is found in so many countries, due largely to its ability to migrate long distances and its very wide range of possible caterpillar food plants. It is seen in the USA from spring to the onset of winter in the north, and all the year round in the south (the numbers of which are largely the result of mass migrations from Mexico and the one or more resultant generations in the USA). It has no hibernation stage and cannot survive the cold of winter.

PEARLY CRESCENTSPOT *Phyciodes tharos*

Group: Nymphalids
This butterfly can be seen in most of the USA except the Pacific Coast regions. In the south it flies all the year but in the northern parts is on the wing from mid–spring to late autumn. The adult has more rounded front wings than other fritillaries, but has the same orange–brown upper surface, with many dark lines and patches. There is a quite broad dark margin to both the front and hindwings, and the latter has a band of dark spots just above this margin.

The eggs are laid on asters, and the caterpillars are dark with some yellow spots and bands, and black spines along the body. In warmer areas there may be several generations per year, and in colder regions where the species overwinters this is as the partly grown caterpillar.

PIPEVINE BUTTERFLY *Battus philenor*

Group: Papilionids
This is named after the caterpillar food plants – pipevines being members of the genus *Aristolochia*. The majority of these are tender perennial climbers, but some are capable of withstanding frost, usually their underground parts. There are several species of pipevine that are cultivated in gardens and these have no doubt helped

▲ *Vanessa cardui* **is most easily distinguished from the American painted lady by the presence of more than two eyespots on the lower side of the hindwing.**

the butterfly become quite common. The pipevines are poisonous plants and the adults are distasteful to birds because of substances accumulated by the caterpillars as they feed. Because the adults are distasteful several other species of butterfly, which do not have caterpillars that feed on the pipevines and are themselves palatable to birds, have evolved to have a similar appearance as a protection against predation.

The butterflies are on the wing from spring to autumn in the more northern parts of their range but in the warmer south may be seen for most of the year. They are almost completely black on the upper surface of the wings, except for some orange spots along the outer margin of the hindwing. There is a bluish sheen to the hindwings that shows well under some conditions of light. The caterpillars are dark brown or black with a couple of rows of red stubby tubercles along the back. The overwintering stage is the chrysalis.

SILVER-SPOTTED SKIPPER
Epargyreus clarus

Group: Hesperiids

A predominantly brown skipper that gets its English name from the large silvery patch on the underside of the hindwing. It is found in most areas of the USA – all the year round in the south, and from spring to autumn in the north. There may be only one generation in the north, but up to four further south.

The eggs are laid on a wide range of plants, mostly in the plant family Papilionaceae, including trees such as locust (*Robinia pseudoacacia*), wisterias, beans (*Phaseolus* species) and many others. The caterpillars are yellowish green with a red–brown head. They are capable of overwintering in shelters made by tying leaves of the food plant together with silk, and when they pupate it is generally among leaf litter on the ground.

SLEEPY ORANGE *Eurema nicippe*

Group: Pierids

Although not particularly sleepy, it is certainly orange, edged with black on the upperside of the wings. It flies all the year in southern USA. The adults seen further north from spring to late autumn are the result of annual migrations from the south, to replenish the stock because this butterfly cannot survive the cold winter, and there is no hibernating stage. Eggs are laid on clovers and sennas (species of *Senna* and *Cassia*). The caterpillars are green with a stripe along the sides.

SMALL WHITE *Pieris rapae*

Group: Pierids

The small white is found in all parts of the USA, and is often called the European cabbage butterfly, to indicate that it is an introduced species, probably dating from an arrival in North America in 1860.

It is seen from spring to autumn in the north and all the year round in the warmer south. Where it hibernates, this is as a chrysalis. More details of this butterfly can be found in the section on European and United Kingdom butterflies.

SPICEBUSH SWALLOWTAIL *Papilio troilus*

Group: Papilionids

The main colour of the wings is black, with white spots along the outer margins. On the hindwings are some shiny blue spots and a couple of orange ones, with the ones nearest to the tails being essentially eyespots. It is on the wing in the eastern USA from late spring to mid–autumn. The English name is related to the fact that it lays its eggs on the spicebush (*Lindera benzoin*), but it also uses sassafras (*Sassafras albidum*), both of which can be grown in gardens to tempt them from their normal woodland habitat. The caterpillars are green with two pairs of large eyespots at the front end. The overwintering stage is the chrysalis.

▶ **A spicebush swallowtail at a scouring-pad feeding bowl.**

▲ **A male tiger swallowtail in all its striped glory.**

SPRING AZURE *Celastrina ladon*

Group: Lycaenids

This is a very variable butterfly, but the typical form is blue above and greyish on the underside. It is on the wing from early spring to autumn, with the exact times depending on the place, because this butterfly is seen throughout the USA. There is only one brood in the north but two or three in warmer regions.

The males may be seen at mud puddles but the females are more likely to be higher up looking for flowers on which to lay eggs. A wide range of plants is used, including ceanothus, dogwood (*Cornus* species) and viburnum, and these will attract them to gardens. The small caterpillars are greenish through brown to pinkish–brown, and the overwintering stage is the chrysalis.

Did you know?

The dark female swallowtail is considered to be a mimic of the pipevine swallowtail, which is poisonous to most predators. The tiger swallowtail shares its territory with the pipevine swallowtail in the more southerly parts of its range.

TIGER SWALLOWTAIL *Papilio glaucus*

Group: Papilionids

This is a large swallowtail that can be seen on the wing mainly from spring to autumn in all but the western parts of the USA. The upperside of the wings is mostly yellow with broad margins of black, studded with yellow and blue spots close to the tails, as well as a couple of orange–red ones. Extending from the front edge of the front wings are distinct, roughly parallel black streaks stretching into the interior of the wings. Some of the females are almost completely black. The caterpillar food plants include willows, cherries, cottonwood (*Populus deltoides*) and tulip–poplar (*Liriodendron tulipifera*), among others. The mature caterpillars are green with a distinct pair of large eyespots near the head end. The overwintering stage is the chrysalis.

VARIEGATED FRITILLARY *Euptoieta claudia*

Group: Nymphalids

Like many other fritillaries the upper surface of the wings is orange–brown with numerous dark lines covering the basic colour. This is a migrating butterfly that moves north each year to all parts of the USA except the extreme western regions. It cannot overwinter in the north. Although violets are commonly used for egg–laying, the eggs may also be laid on stonecrops *Sedum* species) and passion flowers. The orange–brown body of the caterpillar is marked with black lines and bears numerous black spines.

▲ **The almost unrecognizable dark form of a female tiger swallowtail.**

Adding to the natural population of butterflies is not always easy to do, but if you have caterpillar food plants the adults may lay eggs on them and you can then act as nursemaid to the young ones. Other butterfly enthusiasts could already be breeding some of the common species and may be pleased to help you if the butterflies are not laying on your plants. This chapter shows you how to nurture and protect the developing stages of butterflies for the best results.

Breeding butterflies

Breeding butterflies at home

Plentiful food for caterpillars

THE OBVIOUS first step to breeding any butterfly species is to ensure that you have a very plentiful supply of the caterpillar food plant. First identify the butterflies that visit your garden and make a record of the times when you see them. When you know the names of the butterflies you can look them up in books that deal with your area, and begin to find out on what plants the eggs are laid. For some butterflies there may only be a few plant species to choose, but for others there may be dozens.

If your identification guide tells you whether the butterflies prefer the plants to be grown in the sun or the shade, that will be most useful if you are going to plant them directly in your garden. After all, it is no use growing a plant in a dark shady spot out of sight because it is a 'weed', if the butterflies only ever lay their eggs in full sun. However, you may not really want a stinging nettle in a prime sunny position, but that may be the only place a butterfly will naturally lay its eggs. Also, it may only lay them on young shoots rather than old, tall stems, or perhaps in the centre of large patches rather than a small patch. In any case a small patch may not be enough to feed all the caterpillars that come from a large batch of eggs.

However, just planting the caterpillar food plant, and leaving everything else to Nature, is unlikely to lead to very many adult butterflies. Predators, parasitoids and diseases are likely to take nearly all of the offspring. You may nurture the caterpillars to full size only to discover that they are then the victims of parasitoids. The only way to prevent this is to exclude the adult parasitoids from the food plants as soon as the eggs have been laid.

Protecting the caterpillars

OBVIOUSLY THE form of the plant must be considered but the principle is very simple. Drape very fine mesh netting over the plant on which the eggs are laid, and the subsequent caterpillars will feed. There are suppliers who can provide ready–made nets of the right quality. With large plants or shrubs you may only be able to cover a section. The nets normally have wire hoops sown into them so they do not collapse onto the plant, and they can be open at one end only, so that you can put them over a potted plant or the end of a shoot.

If the nets are open at both ends they are generally called sleeves and can be moved along a stem, a bit at a time, as the caterpillars eat the leaves. The open ends usually have drawstrings so that you can tighten them down onto the pot or stem and prevent parasitoids from getting in. The whole process is called sleeving and is the method that requires minimum effort from you. From time to time you need to open the net and shake out any of the droppings that have accumulated. Many of the ready–made nets have a zip sewn into them along one side so that you can easily open it and let out the frass. Remember to have the zip along the bottom side of the net when you fit it so that the frass drops out. Given time you should end up with some excellent chrysalids hung up inside your net.

You should note that some parasitoids lay their eggs on the plants rather than actually in the butterfly eggs or caterpillars. This can be a problem with plants grown in the open garden before netting, or on plant leaves or shoots taken from outside the garden.

◀ **A netted branch of a tree to protect caterpillars.**

▲ **Protect butterfly eggs from certain predators, by draping a net over a potted plant, and tying it in place.**

▶ **A small potted plant can be put inside a net that has a cardboard disc inserted as a base.**

▲ **A pupa attached to a piece of its food plant that has been cut and put in a damp block of florist's foam.**

Developing chrysalids

IF YOU expect the chrysalids to develop and produce adults within a few weeks, you are best to leave them where they are to emerge. Be aware about whether or not you have any animals around who are able to rip open the netting to get at your butterfly livestock. If there are, or it will be a long time before the adults emerge, you may want to get the chrysalids to a safer place. In most cases they will be attached to the leaves, stems or the net by a silken pad, and for some species a silken girdle around the middle of the chrysalis. If the whole support can be cut out and taken away, that is fine. It can be placed in a protected place, perhaps in a clear plastic container and be held in a reasonable position in, say, a block of florist's wet foam.

If the whole stem with the chrysalids attached cannot be taken, then the chrysalids must be individually removed. The girdles must be cut with a fine pair of scissors. The silk attaching the end of the chrysalis must then be very carefully prized away from whatever it is attached to, leaving as much as possible attached to the chrysalis. It helps to slightly dampen the silk before trying to scrape it off the stems or netting. The removal of a chrysalis should only be done after it has been formed for a few days, and is firm and hard. It is a process that requires a delicate touch.

Once you have a chrysalis loose from its attachments the next stage is to fix it to a thin stick or twig. Place a small drop of a non-toxic glue onto the support you have chosen and let it dry slightly to become tacky. Gently touch the silk at the end of the chrysalis onto the tacky glue and leave it to dry. During this time the support and the chrysalis will be lying on a flat surface. Some chrysalids wriggle quite strongly when handled, so getting a good attachment to the support is essential. When dry the sticks with the chrysalids attached can be placed in a support as described previously or stretched across a support of some kind.

Some chrysalids are formed loose on the ground or in leaf litter and they will not need the careful effort that has just been described. The container with the chrysalids should then be placed in an appropriate place. If the butterfly species is one that overwinters as a chrysalis then the container you have should be exposed to the natural temperatures of the winter period, but not, of course, allowed to get too dry or too wet. If the chrysalids are not exposed to these low temperatures, which they would naturally experience, they may not be able to complete their metamorphosis and all your efforts so far would have been wasted.

Did you know?

If the chrysalis is not attached to something rigid, the adult butterfly may not be able to get out of the chrysalis case when it is ready. If it does not do this completely it may be unable to expand its wings.

▲ **Pupae of the chequered swallowtail, attached by tiny silk threads and glued to a piece of wood.**

Emerging adults

IF THE adults are expected to emerge soon, then again simulate the conditions to which the chrysalids would be naturally exposed. Although they may require warmth they will generally need to be kept out of direct sun, as this may cause them to overheat in the container.

After emergence of the adults, leave them to harden their wings, which may take 24 hours or more, before you let them go. It is fairly obvious when they are ready because they will start to move about and flap their wings. The container can be open and some will fly off. Others may need assistance, so should be individually lifted out and released. This is most easily done when the wings are closed and the butterfly can be picked up gently by the wings and placed on a flower or leaf to get its bearings before flying off.

Rearing caterpillars

Whatever method you use to nurture the caterpillars, do not overcrowd the livestock, as this is almost certain to lead to disease and the death of the whole batch. Until you have gained experience and have the enclosure to expand, just try to rear a few caterpillars at a time.

Other possibilities

IT MAY not be possible to sleeve a plant in the open garden, so instead you could use a potted plant in a container. These containers are generally made from clear plastic and have a lid with lots of air holes in it; you may need to place a piece of fine netting over the top to stop parasitoids getting in.

The plants can be in a small pot, or if you have to use cut plant material it is best placed into damp florist's foam, just as you would with cut flowers. The foam would be in a shallow dish so that you can keep it moist, but you do not want a trough of water in which the caterpillars could drown. This florist's–foam method is generally to be preferred, over keeping the stems in a jar of water. With the latter method, unless you have tightly closed around the neck of the jar with cotton wool, or even better with the type of synthetic wool used in aquarium filters, some of the caterpillars are almost certain to get down into the water and drown.

Another problem that can arise with cut stems directly in water is that the stem and leaves may take up a little too much water for the good of the caterpillars, some of which seem to be harmed or made more susceptible to disease by excessively moist food plants.

▼ **A selection of different-sized plastic containers useful for the butterfly breeder.**

Breeding on a larger scale

AFTER YOU have gained some experience you may feel that you want to breed a larger number of butterflies. This is not practical when you are using small containers, or relying on the few eggs or caterpillars that you can find in the garden or obtain from other people. It is time to consider an altogether larger scale of working.

A large netted enclosure with lots of caterpillar food plants could be one way forward. If you have bred some of your own adults you could let them go at first into your netted enclosure, provided you have also got plenty of flowers for the adults to feed on as well. There you can expect them to pair up and lay eggs on your plants before you let them go into the garden to carry on their free existence.

In general, males need to be a bit older than females for successful mating. Some species will lay almost all their eggs in a few days and so they will have plenty of active life left after they have been released into the garden. Remember that some overwintering adult butterflies do not pair up until the following spring, so you may need to look after them over the winter period.

▽ **Even a small greenhouse can be used to breed successfully a larger number of garden butterflies.**

▲ **Cut shoots of a plant in a jar of water and wet florist's foam.**

▽ **Controlling the temperature by insulation, blinds and automatic window openers is important to provide ideal conditions for butterfly breeding.**

Did you know?

Butterflies get most of their energy from the sugary nectar of flowers. If you do not have enough flowers in the enclosure at the critical time, you can use feeding pads moistened with a dilute solution of sugar water or honey as an alternative to natural feeding. The pads can be of various materials such as plastic pot scourers or synthetic sponges in shallow dishes, or you could construct a more elaborate feeding table with little tubes of sugar solution and imitation flowers around the top to attract the butterflies.

◀ **If you want to have a longer breeding season you may need to extend the daylight hours with special lighting, such as this 400-watt halide lamp.**

The main problem with netted enclosures is making them secure enough to prevent too many parasitoids from entering. A stage further may be to construct a butterfly greenhouse for rearing the young stages. This would allow you to extend the breeding season for some species by providing additional heating and lighting at appropriate times, giving you more generations per year than you would get outside in the garden.

Although you would not be allowed to release any non–indigenous species into your garden, you can learn a great deal about the habits of butterflies of other countries in such a greenhouse, and with attention to detail establish populations of some species that could survive from one year to the next.

This may be the only way in which some tropical or subtropical butterflies can be saved from extinction. Of course, it should be remembered that both the conditions inside the greenhouse, and the plants grown, need adjusting to suit the species of butterfly you are breeding.

▲ **Netting over open windows will prevent dangerous parasitoids from entering a butterfly-breeding greenhouse.**

◀ **Monarchs easily pair up in a protected environment.**

Genetic variation in butterflies

ALL THE individual butterflies in a species are not the same because there are genetic differences between the individuals. Also, the differences between males and females are often so marked that the two sexes were once considered to be different species until the truth was discovered. Sometimes there are seasonal differences in appearance, due to environmental factors such as the temperature at which the caterpillars develop.

The genetic difference in butterflies is a difficult thing to understand, but it can be important. With a mobile species that moves freely from place to place these genetic variations are spread throughout the entire species. Where there are barriers of some sort to movement and interbreeding, then distinct populations within a species can develop. Where they are quite stable and distinct they may be referred to as 'subspecies', which results in a further Latin word, following the specific name.

When the differences are not so great, you may have 'forms' rather than subspecies. This is one of the reasons why it is not recommended that you bring back livestock from another country, even if it is of a species that is common where you live. There may be genetic differences of ecological importance that you do not know about and this could, potentially, upset the genetic make–up of your local population of that species. This, of course, is of less importance with migratory species that only come to your garden from other countries anyway.

The genetic factor

Behavioural or physiological differences occur between individuals, which are due to genetic differences. Preference to lay eggs on a particular food plant can be a genetic instruction, or sometimes due to a non-genetic preference carried over from what the caterpillar fed on before it became an adult.

⏥ **A large cedarwood greenhouse used for breeding butterflies. Breeding must be carried out with an understanding of wildlife legislation.**

Laws relating to butterflies

BREEDING THE common butterflies that visit your garden is an enjoyable and rewarding experience. However, if you wish to become seriously involved in breeding rare and endangered species, or ones that are present on someone else's land and not your own, there are certain things that must be considered before you rush out and try your new skills out on those butterflies.

The first consideration must always be whether or not it is legal to breed and release your chosen species. There are very many pieces of legislation that relate to wildlife, including butterflies. Each country and even each state or its equivalent within a country will have appropriate laws. A few of these laws are accepted by virtually all countries, such as the CITES laws. Others relate to only a particular country or state.

Departments concerned with agriculture and forestry administer laws relating to wildlife. Changes to the laws are made at quite frequent but often irregular intervals, and it is essential to get the latest information. However, reading the statutes can be a difficult task for the ordinary person due to the use of legal jargon. Fortunately, it is very unlikely that any of the species of butterflies mentioned in such documents will be ones that come to your garden.

▲ **If you want to study butterflies that do not naturally occur in your region, or which are specially protected, it is essential to have netted windows and doors to prevent escapes.**

Almost all butterflies on protected lists are there because they are confined to a very few localities and occur in very small numbers, and so are thought to be in need of protection. It is easy to pass conservation laws and create long lists of butterflies that become illegal to possess, dead or alive, but just how valuable these laws are in saving those butterflies from extinction is a matter of some debate. Such laws are, of course, essential in preventing the illegal trade in protected species.

Unfortunately, those who are required to enforce the laws as they apply to specific countries rarely know enough to positively identify all stages of the life cycles of protected species, and this can lead to serious delays. It can also hamper the legitimate activities of individual amateur butterfly enthusiasts who have made, and still are making, major contributions to knowledge.

Also, the laws are usually phrased in such a way that they generally relate to individuals in possession of protected species, and not to those who destroy (sometimes legally) whole habitats in the name of progress or profit. Another and less obvious problem that can arise with protectionist laws concerns the release sites.

It may become almost impossible for butterfly enthusiasts to breed up large numbers of a protected species and release them into a suitable habitat, simply because the problems and costs of looking after the site following the butterflies' release can be too great. Fortunately in some countries, such as the UK, there is extensive co-operation between amateur breeders, conservation societies or trusts and governmental bodies, in attempts to re-establish threatened species.

Understanding the law

The laws can be divided into two main types. First, there are those concerned with the conservation of butterflies that are becoming less common and in need of protection. The laws relating to these are administered by departments concerned with conservation and the environment.

The second legal category relates to prohibited species, which may be regarded as pests. Here we could have a species already present in a country, and in such numbers that it is considered a serious pest, and steps are being taken to reduce its numbers. Alternatively, perhaps a species does not currently exist in a country as part of its natural fauna, but if it was introduced could become a serious pest.

Although the adult butterfly is the stage of the life cycle that gives most pleasure to the gardener, how successfully it gets to adulthood depends on the successful passage through the caterpillar stage. Even if you are not thinking of breeding, you should be aware of caterpillars and their food plants. If you want to breed butterflies you need to know which are the favoured plants for egg-laying. This chapter covers lists of caterpillar food plants in major countries, plants not readily available in your own garden.

Plants for caterpillars

The uses of plants

Plants for feeding and egg-laying

SOME BUTTERFLY species can only use one species of plant for egg–laying and the caterpillars will only eat that plant species. These are called monophagous. Other butterfly species lay eggs on a wide range of plants that their caterpillars eat. These caterpillars are called polyphagous, and include many of the butterflies that visit our gardens. You should be aware that not all caterpillars turn into butterflies; some turn into moths and there are a few other insects that have young leaf–eating stages.

When lists of caterpillar food plants for a butterfly species are offered, there may be several different genetic strains of that butterfly species, only some of which will eat a particular plant species. Also, butterflies can sometimes lay eggs on plants that are not caterpillar food plants at all, or which may only be able to support the caterpillars for a few stages in their growth. The separate stages of a caterpillar's growth are called instars, and are separated by a skin change as the caterpillar grows larger. Often the instars can look completely different from one another.

▼ **Many caterpillars you see may not be those of butterflies. This is one of a day-flying cinnabar moth.**

▲ **Even growing weeds, like docks, in pots can be difficult. This one has been eaten by caterpillars of the small copper.**

Growing food plants that are normally growing wild outside the garden is often more difficult than growing cultivated garden plants. The exact environmental conditions necessary cannot always be duplicated in the garden. If you try and grow even common garden weeds to a large size in pots of garden soil, you need to start early, long before you need them as food plants for the caterpillars. Consult books on the native flora of your area to get some idea of the preferred soil, moisture and climatic conditions required. Also, make contact with other butterfly enthusiasts who are already growing the plants in question.

Wild plants for butterflies

WITH THE lists that follow, you will be leaving the safe confines of your garden, where the plants are well known and well documented. Instead, you'll be entering the countryside of the lepidopterist (one who studies butterflies and moths). Here, almost all the plants are wild. They are unlikely to be available from usual garden plant suppliers, and it may even be difficult to find mention of them in gardening books. You should, however, be able to more easily cross–refer these plants with those mentioned in other butterfly books.

We have attempted to include butterflies that occur in major countries worldwide. Therefore, you will not find in your area some of the listed plants, simply because they do not grow naturally there.

The following lists of caterpillar food plants are not complete for every species, nor do they indicate that every genetic strain of a butterfly species will eat every plant included.

▼ **Not every pretty caterpillar you find will turn into a butterfly. This one will produce a vapourer moth.**

Directory of plants for caterpillars

DANAIDS

Lesser Wanderer (Australia)
Danaus chrysippus

ASCLEPIADACEAE

- *Asclepias curassavica*
- *Asclepias fruticosa*
- *Asclepias rotundifolia*
- *Calotropis gigantea*
- *Calotropis procera*
- *Cynanchum floribundum*
- *Ischnostemma carnosum*
- *Stapelia grandiflora*
- *Stapelia variegata*

Monarch (Australia, Europe, New Zealand, North America)
Danaus plexippus

Polyphagous within the family Asclepiadaceae

ASCLEPIADACEAE

- *Araujia hortorum*
- *Asclepias* species
- *Calotropis gigantea*
- *Matelea laevis*
- *Matelea reticulata*
- *Sarcostemma clausa*
- *Stapelia grandiflora*
- *Stapelia variegata*
- other species in the family Asclepiadaceae

Plain Tiger (Europe, New Zealand, North America)

HELICONIDS

Gulf Fritillary (North America)
Agraulis vanillae

PASSIFLORACEAE

- *Passiflora x belotii*
- *Passiflora caerulea*
- *Passiflora edulis*
- *Passiflora foetida*
- *Passiflora incarnata*
- *Passiflora ligularis*
- *Passiflora manicata*
- *Passiflora suberosa*
- other species in the family Passifloraceae

▷ **Passiflora x belotii**, the leaves of which are used as food by the caterpillars of the gulf fritillary.

▽ **Passiflora foetida**, an odd-smelling passionflower, is used by the gulf fritillary.

HESPERIIDS

Checkered Skipper (North America) *Pyrgus communis*

MALVACEAE

- *Abutilon theophrasti*
- *Alcea rosea*
- *Althaea officinalis*
- *Callirhoe leiocarpa*
- *Hibiscus trionum*
- *Malvastrum rotundifolia*
- *Modiola caroliniana*
- other species in the family Malvaceae

Doubleday's Skipper (Australia)
Toxidia doubledayi

POACEAE

- Unidentified grasses

Fiery Skipper (North America)
Hylephila phyleus

POACEAE

- *Axonopus compressus*
- *Cynodon dactylon*
- *Digitaria sanguinalis*
- *Eragrostis hypnoides*
- *Paspalum conjugatum*
- *Poa pratensis*
- *Saccharum officinarum*
- *Stenotaphrum secundatum*

Phigalia Skipper (Australia)
Trapezites phigalia

LOMANDRACEAE

- *Lomandra filiformis*

Silver-Spotted Skipper
(North America) *Epargyreus clarus*

MIMOSACEAE

- *Acacia* species

PAPILIONACEAE

- *Astragalus* species
- *Desmodium* species
- *Lathyrus palustris*
- *Phaseolus vulgaris*
- *Robinia* species
- *Wisteria frutescens*
- *Wisteria sinensis*
- and other species in the
  family Papilionaceae

Small Skipper (Europe)
Thymelicus sylvestris

POACEAE

- *Brachypodium pinnatum*
- *Brachypodium sylvaticum*
- *Holcus lanatus*
- *Holcus mollis*
- *Phleum pratense*

Yellow-Banded Dart (Australia)
Ocybadistes walkeri

PHORMIACEAE

- *Dianella* species

POACEAE

- *Brachypodium distachyon*
- *Cynodon dactylon*
- *Pennisetum clandestinum*
- *Thuarea involuta*

LYCAENIDS

Common Blue (New Zealand)
Zizina labradus

PAPILIONACEAE

- *Desmodium* species
- *Glycine* species
- *Lotus australis*
- *Macroptilium lathyroides*
- *Medicago* species
- *Phaseolus vulgaris*
- *Pisum sativum*
- *Psoralea adscendens*
- *Psoralea patens*
- *Trifolium* species
- *Vicia faba*
- *Virgilia oroboides*
- and other species in the
  family Papilionaceae

Common Copper
(New Zealand)
Lycaena salustius

POLYGONACEAE

- *Muehlenbeckia* species

◀ **Grassy places are
the haunts of the small
skipper.**

Dark-Banded Copper
(New Zealand) *Chrysophanus enysii*

POLYGONACEAE

* *Muehlenbeckia* species

Geranium Bronze (Europe)
Cacyreus marshalli

GERANIACEAE

* *Geranium* species
* *Pelargonium* species and cultivars

Gray Hairstreak (North America)
Strymon melinus

A very polyphagous species, but often only one or two plant species are used in a particular family. Where this is the case only the family name is given.

AGAVACEAE

APOCYNACEAE

ARECACEAE

ASCLEPIADACEAE

BIGNONIACEAE

BORAGINACEAE

CACTACEAE

CAESALPINIACEAE

* *Cassia alata*
* *Cassia puberula*

▶ **Ivy growing over holly provides two food plants for the holly blue at different times of the year.**

CRASSULACEAE

EBENACEAE

ERICACEAE

EUPHORBIACEAE

* *Croton capitatus*
* *Croton monanthogynus*
* *Eremocarpus setigerus*

FAGACEAE

HYPERICACEAE

JUGLANDACEAE

LAMIACEAE

* *Hyptis emoryi*
* *Lamium amplexicaule*
* *Salvia mellifera*

LOASACEAE

MALVACEAE

* *Callirhoe leiocarpa*
* *Gossypium herbaceum*
* *Hibiscus* species
* *Malva* species
* *Sida hederacea*
* *Sphaeralcea ambigua*

MORACEAE

MYRICACEAE

PAPILIONACEAE

* *Amorpha* species
* *Amphicarpa* species
* *Astragalus* species
* *Desmodium* species
* *Glycyrrhiza lepidota*
* *Indigofera texana*
* *Lespedeza* species
* *Lupinus* species
* *Medicago sativa*
* *Melilotus alba*
* *Phaseolus* species
* *Pisum sativum*
* *Sesbania drummondi*
* *Trifolium* species
* *Vigna sinensis*

PINACEAE

POACEAE

POLYGONACEAE

* *Eriogonum* species
* *Polygonum* species
* *Rumex salicifolius*

RHAMNACEAE

ROSACEAE

* *Crataegus* species
* *Eriobotrya japonica*
* *Malus pumila*
* *Rosa californica*
* *Rubus idaeus*

RUTACEAE

SCROPHULARIACEAE

VERBENACEAE

ZYGOPHYLLACEAE

Holly Blue (Europe)
Celastrina argiolus

AQUIFOLIACEAE

• *Ilex aquifolium*

ARALIACEAE

• *Hedera helix*

CELASTRACEAE

• *Euonymus europaeus*

CORNACEAE

• *Cornus sanguinea*

PAPILIONACEAE

• *Sarothamuns scoparius*
• *Ulex europaeus*

RHAMNACEAE

• *Frangula alnus*

ROSACEAE

• *Rubus fruticosus* aggregate
  (the term 'aggregate' here
  means that the *Rubus* species
  mentioned is a single name
  used to cover a group of very
  similar plants, regarded by
  some as separate species).

◄ **Gorse is sometimes a food plant for the holly blue.**

Pea Blue (Australia)
or Long-Tailed Blue (Europe)
Lampides boeticus

PAPILIONACEAE

• *Chamaecytisus prolifer*
• *Clianthus formosus*
• *Colutea arborescens*
• *Crotolaria* species
• *Dolichos* species
• *Kennedia prostrata*
• *Lathyrus* species
• *Lotus australis*
• *Lupinus* species
• *Phaseolus vulgaris*
• *Pisum sativum*
• *Psoralea patens*
• *Sarothamnus scoparius*
• *Sesbania cannabina*
• *Spartium junceum*
• *Swainsona* species
• *Ulex europaeus*
• *Vicia faba*
• *Vicia sativa*
• *Virgilia oroboides*

Small Copper (Europe)
or American Copper
(North America) *Lycaena phlaeas*

POLYGONACEAE

• *Oxyria digyna*
• *Polygonum* species
• *Rumex acetosa*
• *Rumex acetosella*
• *Rumex crispus*

▼ **Some caterpillars of the small copper have distinct reddish sides whereas others remain plain green.**

▲ **You need good eyesight to spot eggs of the small or American copper.**

Small Copper (New Zealand)
Lycaena boldenarum

POLYGONACEAE

• *Muehlenbeckia* species

Spring Azure (North America)
Celastrina ladon

A very polyphagous species but often only one or two plant species are used in a particular family. Where this is the case only the family name is usually given unless a particular species is commonly used.

ACERACEAE

ANACARDIACEAE

AQUIFOLIACEAE

ARALIACEAE

• *Aralia elata*
• *Aralia hispida*

ASTERACEAE

• *Actinomeris alternifolia*
• *Chrysanthemum leucanthemum*
• *Helianthus* species
• *Verbesina helianthoides*

CAPRIFOLIACEAE

• *Lonicera sempervirens*
• *Viburnum* species

CORNACEAE

• *Cornus* species

ERICACEAE

• *Ledum palustre*
• *Vaccinium corymbosum*

FAGACEAE

HIPPOCASTANACEAE

• *Aesculus californica*

LAMIACEAE

MORACEAE

OLEACEAE

PAPILIONACEAE

• *Apios americana*
• *Crotalaria sagittalis*
• *Erythrina* species
• *Lotus scoparius*
• *Lupinus* species
• *Melilotus officinalis*

RANUNCULACEAE

RHAMNACEAE

• *Ceanothus* species

ROSACEAE

• *Adenostoma fasciculatum*
• *Chamaebatiaria millefolium*
• *Holodiscus* species
• *Malus pumila*
• *Peraphyllum* species
• *Physocarpus monogynus*
• *Prunus* species
• *Rubus* species
• *Spiraea salicifolia*

SAXIFRAGACEAE

▶ **The spring azure sometimes uses *Rhus typhina* as a food plant.**

NYMPHALIDS

American Painted Lady
(North America) *Vanessa virginiensis*

A polyphagous species mostly using plants in the family Asteraceae, and only one or two species in the other families listed.

ASTERACEAE

- *Anaphalis margaritacea*
- *Antennaria* species
- *Arctium lappa*
- *Artemesia* species
- *Carduus* species
- *Cirsium arvense*
- *Gnaphalium* species
- *Helianthus* species
- *Onopordum acanthium*
- *Silybum marianum*
- *Senecio* species
- *Vernonia* species

BALSAMINACEAE

BORAGINACEAE

- *Echium vulgare*
- *Myosotis* species

MALVACEAE

- *Alcea rosea*
- *Malva* species

PAPILIONACEAE

SCROPHULARIACEAE

URTICACEAE

Australian Painted Lady
(Australia, New Zealand)
Vanessa kershawi

ASTERACEAE

- *Ammobium alatum*
- *Arctotheca calendula*
- *Artemesia* species
- *Gnaphalium* species
- *Helichrysum bracteatum*
- *Helichrysum* species
- *Helipterum roseum*
- *Onopordum acanthium*

LAMIACEAE

- *Lavandula angustifolia* (syn. *L. officinalis*)

Buckeye (North America)
Junonia coenia

ACANTHACEAE

- *Dyschoriste linearis*
- *Ruellia nudiflora*
- *Ruellia runyonii*

PLANTAGINACEAE

- *Plantago* species

SCROPHULARIACEAE

- *Antirrhinum majus*
- *Buchnera floridana*
- *Castilleja purpurea*
- *Cymbalaria muralis*
- *Digitalis* species
- *Gerardia* species
- *Kickxia spuria*
- *Linaria* species
- *Maurandya antirhinifolia*
- *Orthocarpus* species
- *Penstemon azureus*
- *Russelia equisetiformis*
- *Seymeria cassioides*
- *Veronica* species

VERBENACEAE

- *Lippia* species

▶ The weed *Plantago major* is just one of the food plants for the buckeye.

◄ **Commas pairing in a butterfly greenhouse.**

▶ **One of many *Ruellia* species, food plants for the common eggfly.**

▲ **Comma caterpillars on hop leaves.**

▲ ***Portulaca grandiflora*, a possible food plant for the common eggfly.**

Comma (European)
Polygonia c-album

CANNABACEAE

- *Humulus lupulus*

GROSSULARIACEAE

- *Ribes* species

ULMACEAE

- *Ulmus* species

URTICACEAE

- *Urtica dioica*

Common Eggfly (Australia)
Hypolimnas bolina

ACANTHACEAE

- *Asystasia* species
- *Pseuderanthemum variabile*
- *Ruellia* species

AMARANTHACEAE

ASTERACEAE

MALVACEAE

POLYGONACEAE

PORTULACACEAE

RUBIACEAE

Great Spangled Fritillary
(North America) *Speyeria cybele*

VIOLACEAE

- *Viola* species

Map Butterfly (Europe)
Araschnia levana

URTICACEAE

- *Urtica dioica*

Meadow Argus (Australia)
Junonia villida

CONVOLVULACEAE

GENTIANACEAE

GOODENIACEAE

- *Goodenia* species
- *Scaevola aemula*

PLANTAGINACEAE

- *Plantago* species

SCROPHULARIACEAE

- *Antirrhinum* species
- *Russelia equisetiformis*

VERBENACEAE

- *Verbena* species

The map butterfly lays strings of eggs on stinging nettle leaves.

Nettle-Tree Butterfly (Europe)
Libythea celtis

ULMACEAE

- *Celtis australis*

Painted Lady (Europe, North America) *Vanessa cardui*

One of the most polyphagous species in the world. A complete list of food plants would be very long. Mostly plants in the Asteraceae are used. Families with only one or a few food plants are just listed by family.

APIACEAE

ASTERACEAE

- *Achillea millefolium*
- *Anaphalis margaritacea*
- *Arctium* species
- *Artemesia* species
- *Calendula officinalis*
- *Carduus* species
- *Carlina vulgaris*
- *Centaurea* species
- *Chrysanthemum* species
- *Cirsium* species
- *Cnicus benedictus*
- *Cynara scolymus*
- *Filago* species
- *Helianthella* species
- *Helianthus* species
- *Helichrysum* species
- *Lactuca sativa*
- *Lappa officinalis*
- *Onopordon acanthium*
- *Parthenium argentatum*
- *Senecio* species
- *Silybum marianum*
- *Wyethia glabra*
- *Xanthium pennsylvanicum*

The painted lady frequently lays eggs on troublesome thistle weeds.

BORAGINACEAE

- *Amsinckia douglasiana*
- *Anchusa officinalis*
- *Borago officinalis*
- *Cryptantha angustifolia*
- *Echium vulgare*
- *Symphytum officinale*

BRASSICACEAE

CHENOPODIACEAE

CONVOLVULACEAE

CUCURBITACEAE

HYDROPHYLLACEAE

LAMIACEAE

Echium vulgare, a possible food plant for the painted lady.

MALVACEAE

- *Althaea* species
- *Malva* species
- *Sida hederacea*
- *Sphaeralcea ambigua*

PAPILIONACEAE

- *Glycina max*
- *Lupinus* species
- *Medicago sativa*
- *Phaseolus vulgaris*
- *Pisum sativum*
- *Trifolium* species

PLANTAGINACEAE

POACEAE

POLYGONACEAE

RHAMNACEAE

ROSACEAE

RUTACEAE

SOLANACEAE

ULMACEAE

URTICACEAE

- *Urtica* species

VERBENACEAE

Peacock (European)
Inachis io

CANNABINACEAE

- *Humulus lupulus*

URTICACEAE

- *Urtica dioica*

▲ The flowers of the male hop plant *Humulus lupulus* are very different from those of the female.

Pearly Crescentspot or Pearl Crescent (North America)
Phyciodes tharos

ASTERACEAE

- *Aster* species

Queen of Spain Fritillary (European) *Issoria lathonia*

BORAGINACEAE

- *Borago officinalis*

PAPILIONACEAE

- *Onobrychis viciifolia*

VIOLACEAE

- *Viola* species

▼ There are many species and cultivars of violets, the leaves of which are eaten by the caterpillars of several different fritillaries.

◀ Caterpillars of the painted lady, feeding on a patch of nettle leaves.

Red Admiral (Europe)
Vanessa atalanta

URTICACEAE

- *Parietaria judiaca*
- *Urtica dioica*
- *Urtica urens*

Red Admiral (New Zealand)
Vanessa gonerilla

URTICACEAE

- *Urtica dioica*

Small Tortoiseshell (Europe)
Aglais urticae

URTICACEAE

- *Urtica dioica*
- *Urtica urens*

Variegated Fritillary
(North America) *Euptoieta claudia*

Uses plants from several families, but often only a select few species.

ASCLEPIADACEAE

CRASSULACEAE

- *Sedum* species

LINACEAE

- *Linum* species

MENISPERMACEAE

NYCTAGINACEAE

PASSIFLORACEAE

- *Passiflora* species

PLANTAGINACEAE

TURNERACEAE

VIOLACEAE

- *Hybanthus verticillatus*
- *Viola* species

Yellow Admiral (Australia, New Zealand) *Vanessa itea*

URTICACEAE

- *Soleirolia soleirolii*
- *Urtica incisa*
- *Urtica urens*

▼ **Small tortoiseshell caterpillars clustered together on nettle.**

▲ **Rue is a food plant for some caterpillars but the plant can blister the skin if handled in sunlight.**

PAPILIONIDS

Anise Swallowtail
(North America) *Papilio zelicaon*

APIACEAE

- *Anethum graveolens*
- *Angelica* species
- *Apium graveolens*
- *Carum carvi*
- *Cicuta maculata*
- *Conioselinum scopulorum*
- *Daucus* species
- *Foeniculum vulgare*
- *Harbouria trachypleura*
- *Heracleum* species
- *Ligusticum* species
- *Lomatium* species
- *Oenanthe sarmentosa*
- *Pastinaca sativa*
- *Perideridia* species
- *Petroselinum crispum*
- *Pimpinella* species
- *Pseudocymopteris montanus*
- *Pteryxia* species
- *Sphenosciadium capitellatum*
- *Tauschia* species
- *Zizia aptera*

RUTACEAE

- *Citrus* species
- *Ruta graveolens*

Black Swallowtail
(North America) *Papilio polyxenes*

APIACEAE

- *Anethum graveolens*
- *Angelica* species
- *Apium graveolens*
- *Berula erecta*
- *Carum carvi*
- *Cicuta* species
- *Conium maculatum*
- *Cryptotaenia canadensis*
- *Cymopteris panamintensis*
- *Daucus* species
- *Foeniculum vulgare*
- *Harbouria trachypleura*
- *Heracleum maximum*
- *Levisticum officinale*
- *Ligusticum scoticum*
- *Osmorhiza longistylis*
- *Oxypolis canbyi*
- *Pastinaca sativa*
- *Petroselinum crispum*
- *Ptilimnium capillaceum*
- *Sium suave*
- *Spermolepis divaricata*
- *Taenidia integerrima*
- *Tauschia* species
- *Thaspium bar binode*
- *Zizia* species

RUTACEAE

- *Dictamnus albus*
- *Ruta graveolens*
- *Thamnosma* species

Chequered Swallowtail
(Australia) *Papilio demoleus*

RUTACEAE

- *Citrus* species
- *Microcitrus australis* (native orange)

▼ **Caterpillars of the chequered swallowtail.**

▲ *Ptelea trifoliata* has sweetly
scented flowers that attract some
species of swallowtail to lay eggs.

▲ The very different-looking sexes
of the orchard swallowtail paired up
on netting in a butterfly greenhouse.

Orchard Swallowtail
(Australia) *Papilio aegeus*

LAURACEAE

PAPILIONACEAE

- *Psoralea* species

Giant Swallowtail
(North America) *Papilio cresphontes*

PIPERACEAE

RUTACEAE

- *Amyris elemifera*
- *Casimiroa edulis*
- *Choisya* species
- *Citrus* species
- *Dictamnus albus*
- *Ptelea trifoliata*
- *Ruta graveolens*
- *Zanthoxylum* species

STAPHYLEACEAE

RUTACEAE

- *Choisya ternata*
- *Citrus* species
- *Clausena brevistyla*
- *Eriostemon myoporoides*
- *Fagara* species

- *Flindersia* species
- *Geijera parviflora*
- *Halfordia* species
- *Melicope erythrococca*
- *Microcitrus* species
- *Micromelum minutum*
- *Murraya koenigii*
- *Phebalium* species
- *Zanthoxylum brachyacanthum*
- *Zieria* species

▷ The orchard swallowtail eats
leaves of the evergreen Mexican
orange blossom (*Choisya ternata*).

Pipevine Swallowtail
(North America) *Battus philenor*

ARISTOLOCHIACEAE

- *Aristolochia* species

Scarce Swallowtail (Europe)
Iphiclides podalirius

ROSACEAE

- *Malus domestica*
- *Prunus* species
- *Pyrus communis*

Spicebush Swallowtail
(North America) *Papilio troilus*

LAURACEAE

- *Cinnamonum camphora*
- *Lindera benzoin*
- *Persea borbonia*
- *Sassafras albidum*

MAGNOLIACEAE

- *Liriodendron tulipifera*
- *Magnolia virginiana*

Tiger Swallowail (North America)
Papilio glaucus

Not all subspecies will eat all of these plants, but the species as a whole is polyphagous. Where only one or two species are used as food plants, only the plant family name is given.

ACERACEAE

BETULACEAE

- *Alnus* species
- *Betula* species
- *Carpinus caroliniana*
- *Corylus* species

BIGNONIACEAE

FAGACEAE

JUGLANDACEAE

LAURACEAE

- *Cinnamomum camphora*
- *Lindera benzoin*
- *Persea americana*
- *Sassafras albidum*

MAGNOLIACEAE

- *Liriodendron tulipifera*
- *Magnolia* species

OLEACEAE

- *Fraxinus* species
- *Syringa vulgaris*

PLATANACEAE

ROSACEAE

- *Amelanchier canadensis*
- *Crataegus* species
- *Cydonia oblonga*
- *Malus pumila*
- *Prunus* species
- *Sorbus americana*

RUTACEAE

- *Ptelea* species
- *Zanthoxylum americanum*

SALICACEAE

- *Populus* species
- *Salix* species

TILIACEAE

ULMACEAE

◀ **Pipevine flowers can be a few centimetres long.**

▶ **Pipevine flowers Aristolochia can be as large as 12in (30cm) or more.**

PIERIDS

Black-Veined White (Europe)
Aporia crataegi

ROSACEAE

- *Crataegus laevigata*
- *Prunus spinosa*
- *Prunus species*

Brimstone (Europe)
Gonepteryx rhamni

RHAMNACEAE

- *Frangula alnus*
- *Rhamnus cathartica*

▼ **A cultivated *Cleome* species popular and easily grown from seed.**

Caper White (Australia)
Anaphaeis java

CAPPARIDACEAE

- *Apophyllum anomalum*
- *Capparis arborea*
- *Capparis species*
- *Capparis spinosa*

Checkered White
(North America) *Pontia protodice*

BRASSICACEAE

- *Arabis species*
- *Barbarea vulgaris*
- *Brassica species*
- *Cakile edentula*
- *Capsella bursa-pastoris*
- *Cardaria draba*
- *Caulanthus species*
- *Descurainia species*
- *Lepidium species*
- *Lobularia maritima*
- *Raphanus sativus*
- *Rorippa curvisiliqua*
- *Selenia aurea*
- *Sisymbrium altissimum*
- *Thelypodium species*
- *Thlaspi arvense*

CAPPARIDACEAE

- *Cleome species*
- *Wislizenia refralta*

RESEDACEAE

▶ **One of the many species of *cassia*.**

Clouded Sulphur or Common Sulphur (North America)
Colias philodice

PAPILIONACEAE

- *Astragalus species*
- *Baptisia tinctoria*
- *Hedysarum boreale*
- *Lathyrus leucanthus*
- *Lotus species*
- *Lupinus perennis*
- *Medicago species*
- *Melilotus alba*
- *Pisum sativum*
- *Robinia pseudacacia*
- *Thermopsis divaricarpa*
- *Trifolium species*
- *Vicia species*

Clouded Yellow (European)
Colias croceus

PAPILIONACEAE

- *Lotus corniculatus*
- *Medicago sativa*
- *Melilotus officinalis*

- *Trifolium species*

Cloudless Sulphur
(North America) *Phoebis sennae*

CAESALPINIACEAE

• *Cassia* species

PAPILIONACEAE

• *Crotalaria agatifolia*

Green-Veined White (Europe)
Pieris napi

BRASSICACEAE

• *Alliaria petiolata*
• *Armoracia rusticana*
• *Barbarea vulgaris*
• *Brassica napus*
• *Cardamine pratensis*
• *Hesperis matronalis*
• *Nasturtium officinale*
• *Sinapis arvensis*
• *Sisymbrium officinale*

Large White or Cabbage White
(Europe) *Pieris brassicae*

BRASSICACEAE

• *Brassica* species
• *Lunaria annua*
• *Raphanus sativus*

RESEDACEAE

• *Reseda lutea*
• *Reseda luteola*

TROPAEOLACEAE

• *Tropaeolum majus*

▼ ***Cardamine pratensis*, a food plant for the green-veined white and orange tip.**

▲ **Honesty has attractive flowers as well as being a food plant for the large white and orange tip.**

Orange Tip (Europe)
Anthocharis cardamines

BRASSICACEAE

- *Alliaria petiolata*
- *Barbarea vulgaris*
- *Cardamine pratensis*
- *Hesperis matronalis*
- *Nasturtium officinale*
- *Sinapis arvensis*
- *Sisymbrium officinale*
- *Turritis glabra*

Sleepy Orange or Rambling Orange (North America)
Eurema nicippe

CAESALPINIACEAE

- *Cassia* species

Small White or Cabbage White (Australia, Europe, New Zealand, North America) *Pieris rapae*

BRASSICACEAE

- *Brassica* species
- *Lepidium hyssopifolium*

CAPPARIDACEAE

- *Cleome* species

RESEDACEAE

- *Reseda* species

TROPAEOLACEAE

- *Tropaeolum* species

SATYRIDS

Common Brown (Australia)
Heteronympha merope

POACEAE

- *Brachypodium distachyon*
- *Poa poaeformis*
- *Poa tenera*
- *Themeda australis*
- unidentified grasses

Gatekeeper (Europe)
Pyronia tithonus

POACEAE

- *Agropyron repens*
- *Dactylis glomerata*
- *Lolium perenne*
- *Poa annua*
- *Poa trivialis*
- probably other species in the family *Poaceae*

Rock Ringlet (Australia)
Hypocysta euphemia

POACEAE

- unidentified grasses

◄ **Caterpillars of the small white, on nasturtium leaves.**

There are many things you can do to help butterflies survive the winter. Some, of course, need no help and fly off to warmer climates. Others do not have this innate ability to migrate and may not survive the low temperatures and high rainfall of winter. Such butterflies are normally replaced by fresh adults from warmer places the following season. This chapter shows you how to help butterflies by providing shelter and food for them over the winter period and how to safely preserve chrysalids, caterpillars and eggs in order for them to complete their life cycles the following season.

Over-wintering butterflies

Winter survival

Adults

A T THE end of the normal flight season, adults of hardy species will seek out a sheltered spot and settle down to survive the winter. Before they do this they will probably have been feeding up on the late flowers, sugary saps or rotting autumn fruits.

Before humans constructed buildings the only places these butterflies could go were into dense masses of vegetation, holes in trees and into caves. Species that overwintered in this way tended to have very dark undersides to their wings, or have ragged outlines, like the comma, while their upper surfaces could be very bold. A perfectly still, dark butterfly was unlikely to attract the attention of predators.

When buildings were created, new places for hibernation became available. If windows and doors were left open at the critical times towards the end of autumn, the butterflies would find their own way in and to a suitable spot, generally up in the roof or some other dark place. Peacocks and small tortoiseshells were known to congregate in quite large numbers on the ceilings of spare rooms. In the garden old ivy-covered trees and walls made an ideal place for butterflies to hibernate. Other climbers on the walls of houses and outbuildings provide equally good places for overwintering.

▶ **The red admiral rarely hibernates in the UK and needs special attention to keep it alive over the winter.**

▼ **Leave rotting apples on the ground during autumn for butterflies to feed up on before hibernation.**

▲ **The painted lady cannot survive in areas with cold winters, and new migrants must arrive each year from warmer zones.**

Unfortunately there are far fewer places in modern buildings for successful hibernation to take place:

• Fear of crime has led to increased security, resulting in the windows and doors being shut tight, and sheds are locked up – so the butterflies cannot get in.

• Improved housing has done away with most outside toilets, where the windows were often left open during the day – a favourite unheated spot for butterfly hibernation.

• Central heating inside houses has led to a warmer, less humid atmosphere that is unsuitable for butterfly hibernation because the butterflies are likely to lose too much water and perish.

If you have a suitable shed or other outbuilding it is worth finding a means to leave a narrow, preferably vertical gap for butterflies to get in, whilst excluding larger creatures at the same time. The ideal size for this gap would be around ½–¾in (1–2cm) wide and 4in (10cm) long.

Sometimes butterflies use empty bird-nesting boxes in which to hibernate, but this is probably not the best place for them to use if the birds are likely to return before the butterflies leave.

Butterfly boxes

A butterfly box is constructed simply from planks of rough (unplaned) wood that has been neither painted nor treated with preservatives. The planks should be about 3ft (1m) or so long and about 6in (15cm) wide. Three of these are nailed together to form the back and sides of the box with a suitable hole at the top of the back to allow you to hang the box onto a nail in a wall, tree or post, well above ground level.

It is best if the inside of the butterfly box is left quite rough, perhaps with some bark attached to it. The front of the box needs three or four slits cut into it that are about ½–¾in (1–2cm) wide, and as long as possible. Alternatively, you could make up the front from strips of wood, leaving the appropriate gaps between them. The front should be easily removable. The roof should overlap at the front and slope up from front to back.

A better idea is to provide the butterflies with protective outdoor butterfly boxes for overwintering.

Butterflies will naturally find their way into the box, perhaps coming out on early warm days in spring to feed before going back in again. If you have bred some late-season hibernating species, and have fed them up well, you could try putting them into the box. If they are not ready to hibernate they will easily get out through the slits and may well return when they are ready. These boxes have been around for some years, especially in the USA. Obviously, they will only be of potential use to butterflies that over-winter as adults. Experience as to how successful such boxes are in other parts of the world is unknown.

If you have been breeding a species that does not hibernate naturally in your area because it is too cold, then other overwintering methods can be tried. You will need to keep the butterflies from getting too cold, which generally means keeping the temperature at a minimum of just above freezing, but if too high they will be stimulated into activity. The air must not be too dry or they will lose water and the light should not be too bright or it will stimulate unwanted activity.

▲ **Grow your own unsprayed flowers in pots for winter feeding if you have adult butterflies. This is *Primula obconica*.**

▲ **Three overwintering chequered swallowtails feeding at sugar-water pads. Feed adults like this once a week.**

How to feed at a sugar-water pad

Gently take hold of the butterfly by its closed wings, and allow its feet to just touch the sugary pad – the tips of the feet can sense the presence of sugar. If the butterfly seems loath to uncurl its proboscis to feed, you could try inserting the blunt end of a needle into the open centre of the coiled proboscis and gently unrolling it till the tip reaches the sugar. After a few feeds the butterfly will learn what to do itself. This method is often used to overwinter red admirals in the UK, where they would not normally be able to survive the winter.

▲ **The large white butterfly overwinters as a chrysalis.**

You need to provide a room at a suitable temperature and keep the butterflies in, for example, a netted cylinder similar to those used for sleeving caterpillars onto their food plants, or a small thermostatically regulated plant propagator. You may need to feed the butterflies at least once a week throughout the winter period. There are unlikely to be any nectar-producing garden flowers at this time of year, and florists' blooms are almost certain to have been sprayed with insecticides. This means you will have to make up a dilute solution of honey or sugar water, and then encourage the butterflies to feed. The sugar can be ordinary sucrose but it is better to use fructose (fruit sugar), which is sweeter and has less of a tendency to crystallize. Glucose is the least sweet sugar and therefore the least desirable to use. Feeding is done at the sugar-soaked pad, and the temperature needs to be adequate for the butterfly to be active, say 59–68°F (15–20°C).

You should not overfeed butterflies. You will tell by looking at the butterfly's abdomen (tail section of the body). If it is enlarged, stop feeding.

Chrysalids

WITH SPECIES where the chrysalis is the overwintering stage, there are few difficulties. If you are breeding the butterflies yourself, which is the most likely reason that you have the chrysalids anyway, you just need to give them some protection from potential predators, such as mice or rats, and keep them out of the rain.

If it is not convenient to keep them attached to bits of their food plant, the chrysalids can be taken off and laid on cotton wool or tissue paper in a closed container kept at an appropriate winter temperature. Some find it convenient to put the chrysalids in plastic boxes and to keep them over winter in the salad section of the refrigerator (NOT in a freezer). The ideal temperature is about 41°F (5°C).

When you expect them to be ready to emerge, they can be brought to the outside temperature slowly and attached to sticks for emergence.

Caterpillars

IF CATERPILLARS are the overwintering stage the best option is to leave them where they are, which is usually at the base of the plant. Take steps to prevent too much rain getting to them; this is most easily done if the host plant is growing in a pot.

Usually the caterpillars will start to feed if the temperature warms up, and this may get them out of phase with the natural season, so it is better to keep them only just above freezing (or whatever is the natural temperature) rather than anywhere warmer. If you have caterpillars of a species that does not naturally overwinter in your area, there is no alternative but to keep the temperature warm enough to allow the food plant to grow and the caterpillars to feed. This generally also means extending the hours of daylight through the use of artificial lighting.

▶ **Always keep eggs on the leaf they are laid on.**

Eggs

THERE ARE really only two options if eggs are the overwintering stage. The first is to leave them exactly where they are, and this is suitable for eggs laid onto stems, bark or other solid surfaces that will not shrivel and fall to the ground like the leaves of deciduous plants. The second is to take the material that the eggs are laid on and place it in a more protected place in the same way as we recommended for the chrysalids. Small plastic boxes, in various sizes, can be obtained from entomological suppliers, and these will prove useful both as storage containers, as well as containers in which the very young caterpillars can be fed with a little leaf material until they are large enough to let loose onto plants. To handle such very small caterpillars we recommend the use of a fine artist's paintbrush.

The important thing if you do decide to take charge of eggs is to make sure that you keep a close eye on them because the tiny caterpillars will not survive for long unless they can get at their food plants. For this reason you will certainly not want them to hatch out before the plants are in leaf, so it is important not to keep them in too warm a place.

It is virtually impossible to remove eggs from the surface on which they are laid (stuck is a better word) except for a very few species that have a particularly tough outer coat and a rather low adhesion to the surface. We do not recommend that you try.

Gardeners will be familiar with images of plants and individual flowers, and many will already be taking photographs that appeal to their sense of beauty. Those interested in close-up photography of the natural world are well aware that a slight breeze or the slightest movement of their hands may blur the image. In this chapter you will find out how to successfully take photographs of the natural world including butterflies, caterpillars and tiny eggs, using different types of camera.

Butterfly photography

Capturing butterfly images

History and application

ONE OF the first photographers to obtain images of all the stages of the life cycles of a selection of butterfly species was S. Beaufoy. Published in 1947, his book *Butterfly Lives* is credited with marking the change from collecting the butterflies themselves to photographing them. At that time black and white images were normal for close–up work and camera capabilities for the amateur were rather limited. Now it is much easier to capture the beauty of butterflies, and the possibilities of subsequent image manipulation are extensive.

Images of butterflies are everywhere, from a merely suggestive, single–colour, outline to a full–colour detailed image. They are used for many purposes, such as simple decoration, to create a favourable feeling in potential customers or even for direct personal adornment as tattoos. It is worth remembering that a large proportion of the images of butterflies seen on advertising material is not of any species that will be found in a garden, nor often even in the same country unless one visits tropical butterfly houses.

For the naturalist, the use of butterfly photography in identification guides has had a huge impact. Before cameras, it was the artist who carried out the task of supplying the detailed and accurate images necessary. This tradition still exists today and there are specialist artists whose work can be seen in some of the best butterfly identification guides. Photography can capture very fine detail but it is not always possible to photograph some species with fully extended upper and then the lower surfaces of both front and hind wings as the specialist entomological artist normally does for an identification guide. This may be of great importance in the identification of some species.

Although the painter can reconstruct lifelike poses from observing living butterflies, it is the photographer who has the mastery of the living world, even if lighting conditions may sometimes influence the precise colours of the wings. The good photographer is also an artist, and digital manipulation of the image after it has been captured can extend the photographer's art well beyond what the camera originally captured. A garden photographer will often be looking for the unusual or aesthetic image that captures the ephemeral beauty of butterflies.

Photographing garden butterflies

THE PRINCIPLES of getting good photographs of adult butterflies apply both to inside your garden and when you venture out of it:

1 Learn enough about the species to know when they are likely to be flying in relation to the stages of their life cycle. Some will be seen in the early spring if they have hibernated as adults, such as Small Tortoiseshells or Brimstones in the UK. Others may overwinter in the chrysalis stage and then emerge in the spring as adults. You may expect to see other species for only a few weeks in just one month of the year. Others may have two generations, or even more depending on the weather, in a single year. A few species migrate from a long way away, depending on the weather conditions and population sizes many miles away. For the non–mobile species that form discrete colonies or have very strict environmental requirements you are unlikely ever to see them in your garden.

▶ **Images of butterflies are often used in the media as positive symbols to evoke feelings of beauty and wellbeing.**

2 Butterflies very rarely fly in cold cloudy weather or wet conditions. If the temperature is not high enough they are unable to fly. Many species have dark–coloured bodies to help them absorb as much of the sun's energy as possible. On days that change from sunny to cloudy you can expect butterflies to be flying only in the sunshine. In general the higher the temperature the more active they will be and, incidentally, the more difficult they will be to photograph due to their rapid movements. The structure of the eyes of butterflies means that they do not have very sharp vision but are very good at detecting movement. As you approach, you or your shadow will scare them and they will dart off. A noisy camera autofocus system can also scare them. When visiting inflorescences with many small flowers in them the butterflies may be permanently on the move, especially later in the day when all the nectar has been collected by earlier visitors.

Using an SLR camera

F OR DECADES the only way to capture an image of a butterfly, apart from drawing and painting it, was to use a camera loaded with a light–sensitive film or plate. The light–receptive material consists of chemical pigments distributed in a supporting emulsion and attached to a clear backing. When exposed to light, changes take place in the pigments, which create an invisible, or latent image of the subject. The film/plate must then be removed from the camera and protected from normal daylight until the image has been developed and fixed into a stable state. Only then can the photographer see whether the images are good ones. If the image on the film is a negative one, rather than a slide for direct viewing, a print must then be made, again using special equipment in the darkroom.

All of these stages may take a considerable time, and any poor images represent wasted money and time. Any desired changes needed to the image, even as simple as reducing excessive background space or distracting images, requires careful further darkroom effort. This system

has numerous disadvantages, but despite these and other restrictions excellent results can be obtained with colour films.

The whole process of image capture has changed dramatically over the past decade or so. Enormous developments have taken place in the technology of the digital camera and the ability to carry out post–capture image manipulation. Such is the speed of change that no purpose would be served by illustrating or recommending actual models of cameras or image–processing equipment and methodology. Sufficient to say that the film–based cameras have rapidly become almost obsolete, except for some of those using larger than 35mm film, which is generally the province of professional photographers. The film–based cameras can still be used if the photographer is prepared to accept some of the restrictions noted above and also embrace the advantages of computer–aided, post–image capture, developments.

With the right model of scanner it is possible to convert any traditional photograph, slide or negative into a digital form and then use the same post–image capture computer equipment as a photographer using a digital camera. These digitized images can then be stored in the same

Roosting spots

Late in the year butterflies that are about to hibernate may be so intent on feeding that they are less easily disturbed. Early in the morning before they have fully warmed up from the cold of the night you can often catch a butterfly still hanging with closed wings at its night-time roost. It is worth looking out for such roosting places the evening before, when light may be getting dimmer, but the butterflies are still a little too active to give a good photograph.

space-saving way as any other digital image. Although you might be able to use the lenses from a film camera on a digital camera, a digital camera captures the image in an entirely different way. The individually very small light-sensitive units, or cells, that capture the initial image information in a digital camera are arranged in a grid pattern (an array). Each cell acts like a light meter to generate an electric current. Various systems may be used to distinguish the different colours in the visible spectrum. Each resulting tiny electric current is then amplified and converted into a digit (a number) with each cell, giving rise to a pixel (picture element).

Obviously, the more pixels there are the greater the amount of information that will have been captured about the subject of the photograph. Complex calculations allow an image file to be created that contains the colour distribution in the image. This digital data then has to be organized and written into a temporary storage memory. Image files can be read back as a coloured image on an LCD screen on the camera, put onto removable memory devices and even directly transferred to computers or printers outside of the camera.

One, but by no means the only significant feature of a digital camera is the number of pixels. A megapixel is one million pixels. More pixels do not necessarily mean a better-quality image. The size of the overall sensor chip may also be an important indicator of subsequent image quality, as also is the in-camera data processing capability of the camera itself. There is a huge range of digital cameras available. Check with the actual camera that it has the range of facilities that you want, arranged in a convenient way for you to access them easily, and in a position on the camera that suits your hand size. In the lower price range are various models described as compacts, from entry level to more complex enthusiast's models. The so-called 'prosumer' digital cameras can produce results to professional standards but often not with the interchangeable lenses that are of great value to the specialist photographer.

Moving butterflies

For capturing moving butterflies it is worth looking at models that have improved video facilities. Some can shoot at 50 frames per second or even faster, and still retain the individual stills within the video clip at an adequate quality for individual printing, although if you aim to produce videos rather than still pictures it is well worth looking at suitable dedicated video cameras.

Using flash

A S AN alternative to using a camera with a fast frames per second capability it is possible to stop movement by using flash photography. With close-up (macro) photography the blur caused by wind or hand-held camera shake can be significant and models with image stabilization systems built into them to minimize this problem may be found throughout the whole range of digital cameras. Most cameras come with an in-built flash unit that is normally more than powerful enough for close-up shots of butterflies. The main problem is the likelihood of dark shadows when a single flash is used or the colour-bleaching effect of too bright a flash.

For some of the more expensive SLR models it is possible to buy a ring-flash unit that fits around a macro lens or, more rarely, two or more individual small flash units that can be sited around the lens to give the desired all-round illumination. If you are thinking about going to this level of sophistication, make sure you check for the availability of such specialist flash units before you buy a camera. The keen gardener can capture very good images, within some limitations, without investing a large amount of money on what must be, by the very nature of butterflies, a fleeting opportunity over a restricted seasonal period.

▲ **The colours seen with daylight (left) can be drastically altered when a close flash unit causes reflection from the surface of a butterfly's wings (right).**

Depth of focus

Depth of focus is very important when taking close-up shots of butterflies. Too little and the butterfly, unless it is a right-angle shot of either fully open upper side or fully closed lower side of the wings, will not look its best. Too much depth of focus may well bring in distracting backgrounds that compete for attention with the butterfly. Backgrounds can be faded out, or even completely removed, during image manipulation with suitable software. Trying to fill in out-of-focus parts of a butterfly presents considerable difficulty, but blur can give a sense of movement.

Post-image capture processing

DIGITAL IMAGE manipulation outside of the camera can range from a simple tidying up of the image by reframing to avoid distracting peripheral material to an almost endless selection of features to be found in specialist image–processing packages. It would serve no purpose in this book to elaborate on the actual techniques, which in any case are advancing all the time.

If you have archive material from a film camera or are continuing to use a faithful older non–digital camera that you know well, then the first requirement is a scanner that can digitize your material. Models exist that have the capability to digitize prints, slides and negatives by means of special holders for the material and sufficient resolution to cope with 35mm material. This is where you will need specialist help and a consideration of what you want to do before you buy. Start by consulting an up–to–date book or magazine before you visit a specialist shop or online store. Obviously you will need a laptop or other computer to receive the digital signals from the scanner.

With a digital camera you can print photographs directly by linking it to a digital printer if it has the necessary interface. Some printers are specifically made for this use while others can be general–purpose printers that also link to the computer instead of being just for printing direct from the camera. If the camera has a removable storage memory, you can take this out and replace it with an empty memory so that you can go on taking photographs after the first memory is full. What brand you choose from the many models of printers available depends on what you intend to do. Many shops will have machines where you can print out your photographs without having your own printer, but if you want to store your photographs in digital form you will need the computer and this will normally take in the digital images direct from the camera or removable storage memory via the standard USB connection.

▲ **Keeping this complex background out of focus stops it from competing with the Brimstone butterfly.**

Using colour

The colour of objects around a butterfly can significantly alter the impact of the image. The photographer is lucky if this is a natural event that can be captured directly. With post-capture colour modification, it is sometimes possible to alter the whole visual impact of an image. It is worth gaining an insight into the subject of colour perception to make maximum use of this facility.

Computers normally come with a program that enables you to store the images onto a removable disc, or some other type of external storage. They also enable you to carry out various manipulations and 'improvements' to your original data image. Images can be stored in any number of subject groups and sequences to make retrieval from storage easy. More sophisticated programs can be bought that enable the experienced manipulator of digital images to achieve all manner of special effects, provided your computer has sufficient processing capacity to accept them. As with all things to do with digital photography, take good advice before you buy anything.

When using image–manipulation software remember that the colour you can see on the LCD screen is not necessarily the exact colour you will get when you obtain a paper print from your digital printer. In addition, different inkjet printers with their various combinations of inks, as well as the type of paper used, can affect the printed colours. In general, printing on paper usually gives a duller–looking image than you can see on a screen because printers have a smaller range of reproducible colours than a monitor screen. With computer software you can, however, improve under- or over–exposed photographs, although this may slightly alter the colours.

◁ The rather drab, brownish, underside of this South American heliconid butterfly is dramatically emphasized by the adjacent orange flower on which it is feeding.

▷ This tropical South American clearwing (*Greta oto*) shows the underlying membrane of a butterfly wing because tiny hairs are present instead of the scales on most butterfly wings.

▽ The dark edges to the wings of this female holly blue clearly distinguish it from the male.

The image data originally captured by a digital camera at the analogue to digital conversion gives rise to very large data files that require a great amount of memory space. This is generally known as a RAW file, of which there are several types, and the files usually require too much time and computer processing power to be of use to the ordinary amateur photographer. Because of this problem image data files are generally reduced in size ('compressed') by discarding some of the original data. This can be done in various ways and to different extents, making the files more manageable without any significant loss of picture quality for ordinary photographic purposes. One of the systems commonly used in cameras is known as JPEG, but others also exist. Various levels of compression can be available and the size of the data files can be reduced very significantly, which can save considerable time in transferring images.

The beginner with image manipulation is recommended to study a good recent book on digital photography to clarify their thoughts before starting on serious image manipulation. There are so many possibilities that more time is easily spent at the computer rather than with the camera.

Butterfly wing patterns

The colours on butterfly wing patterns are caused by the presence of tiny scales, which fit into sockets on an underlying, clear, wing membrane. Some colours are due to chemicals in the scales but others, such as the iridescent blues and greens, are due to the presence of very complex scales that refract the light. These scales are tiny in size but if the wing is magnified about x10 or more it will result in a blurring of the pattern edges even when there are enough pixels in the image to allow this amount of magnification.

Further reading

This list is only a selection by the authors from the many excellent books that exist and more are being produced all the time – it is not intended to be comprehensive. Not all the books given in this list may be available at your local bookseller. We suggest that if a title cannot be found as a current edition that you consult your local library who may be able to obtain a copy for you to read. You may also be able to locate a copy via the Internet. There are also specialist booksellers who are able to obtain books for you to purchase that are not available through other sources. Your local butterfly or entomological society may be able to supply the names and addresses of such specialist booksellers.

Butterflies

Baines, V. and Jackson, B. *Mindful of Butterflies*, The Book Guild Ltd, 1999. This large-format book with full-colour paintings by V. Baines explores the butterfly populations of the UK and North America. It also describes the practices and ecology of creating habitats for butterflies.

Beaufoy, S. *Butterfly Lives*, Collins, 1947. This is the original book, illustrated with black and white photographs, that marks the beginnings of close-up photography of the life cycle stages of 22 butterflies that, except for a few species, are still to be seen commonly in the British Isles. The accompanying text is both descriptive of the butterflies and narrative of the circumstances under which the photographs were taken.

Braby, Michael F. *The Complete Field Guide to the Butterflies of Australia*, CSIRO Publishing, 2004. Contains colour photographs of all 416 species and relevant maps.

Brackenbury, J. *Insects in Flight*, Blandford, 1992. Contains exceptional photographs of insects in flight, including some butterflies.

Brooks, M. and Knight, C. *A Complete Guide to British Butterflies*, Jonathan Cape, 1982. The entire life histories of the British species are described and illustrated in colour photographs.

Chinery, M. *Collins Guide to Butterflies: A Photographic Guide to the Butterflies of Britain and Europe*, Harper Collins, 1998. A good field guide with much useful information on the identification, biology and distribution of the butterflies of this area, illustrated with colour photographs of the species. Note that many regional and county butterfly books also exist giving information on the species present.

Common, I.F.B. and Waterhouse, D.F. *Butterflies of Australia*, Angus and Robertson, 1981 (revised edition). The major work dealing with the butterflies, their identification, life histories and biology for Australia.

Cribb, P.W. *Breeding the British Butterflies*, The Amateur Entomologists' Society (UK), 2001 (revised edition). This is volume 18 of The Amateur Entomologist series. A small paperback book that is packed with useful information for those wishing to breed the UK butterflies.

Dennis, J.V. and Tekulsky, M. *How to Attract Hummingbirds and Butterflies*, Ortho Books, Chevron Chemical Company, 1991. A large-format paperback dealing with common USA hummingbirds and butterflies in roughly equal proportions.

Dennis, R.L.H. *Butterflies and Climate Change*, Manchester University Press, 1993. The influence of weather and climate on butterflies is discussed, including the past and probable future effects of climate change.

Dunbar, D. editor, *Saving Butterflies: A Practical Guide to the Conservation of Butterflies*, Butterfly Conservation (UK), 1993. A book dealing with all aspects of the conservation of UK butterflies and the maintenance of their habitats.

Emmel, T. *Butterflies: Their World, Their Life-cycles, Their Behaviour*, Thames and Hudson, 1976. A classic book from a well-known world expert considering aspects of butterfly biology worldwide.

Feltwell, J. *The Conservation of Butterflies in Britain, Past and Present*, Wildlife Matters, 1995. An account of the development and practice of butterfly conservation in one of the countries of the world where the role of butterfly enthusiasts has been most significant.

Fitter, R. *Wildlife for Man: How and Why We Should Conserve Our Species*, Collins, 1986. Still an interesting book with an emphasis towards the human view of the value of conserving species. A source-book from the Species Survival Commission of the International Union for the Conservation of Nature.

Forey, P. and McCormick, S. *Identification Guides: British and European Butterflies*, Flame Tree Publishing, 2007. This innovative book contains a selection of the common and widely distributed butterflies of Europe, including the British Isles. Aimed at the beginner, it combines clear coloured drawings of the species with concise descriptions of the adults, their habitats and distribution, caterpillars and flying periods. These are interspersed with full-page, and closer, photographs of the species to give a book that combines the artistic with the factual.

Fry, R. and Lonsdale, D. editors, *Habitat Conservation for Insects – a Neglected Green Issue*, The Amateur Entomologists' Society, 1991 (Volume 21 of a series). Deals with the conservation of habitats for insects, with much information on the special needs of butterflies, from a UK viewpoint.

Gibbs, G. *New Zealand Butterflies: Identification and Natural History*, Collins, 1980. An account of the rather limited number of species that occur in New Zealand.

Gilbert, P. *Butterfly Collectors and Painters*, Beaumont Publishing, 2000. A collection of some 60 colour plates from the London Natural History Museum's Library Collections.

Goodden, R. and Goodden R. *Butterflies of Britain and Europe*, New Holland, 2002. For over 50 years Robert Goodden has devoted his life to butterflies on a worldwide scale. He is an author of many books, photographer, conservationist and breeder of butterflies.

Hicks, P. *Photographing Butterflies and Other Insects*, Fountain Press, 1997. A good book giving much useful information on using film cameras and techniques for photographing insects, illustrated with many excellent photographs.

Higgins, L.G. and Riley, N.D. *Butterflies of Britain and Europe*, Collins, 1993. Covering the European butterflies, with distribution maps and colour illustrations by B. Hargreaves, this is a useful book for the region.

Lewington, R. *Pocket Guide to Butterflies of Great Britain and Ireland*, British Wildlife Publishing, 2003. Over 600 paintings by one of the finest butterfly painters, showing details that photographs cannot easily give, together with distribution maps.

New, T.R. *Butterfly Conservation*, Oxford University Press, 1992. This deals with all aspects of the conservation of butterflies on a worldwide basis and is the ideal starting point for anyone with a serious interest in the conservation of butterflies.

Newland, D.E. *Discover Butterflies in Britain*, WILDGuides, 2006. For those who want to go outside of their garden this book gives a list of the butterfly reserves and places to find butterflies, with information on over 60 sites as well as the butterfly species.

Pollard, E. and Yates, T.J. *The Monitoring of Butterflies for Ecology and Conservation*, Chapman Hall, 1993. Gives detailed information on a UK butterfly monitoring scheme started in 1976.

Scott, J.A. *The Butterflies of North America*, Stanford University Press, 1992 (second edition). The definitive book on North American butterflies. A must for anyone interested in that area and the biology of the butterflies that live there. Note that many regional and state butterfly books exist giving information on the species present.

Thomas, J.A. *Butterflies of the British Isles*, Hamlyn, 1992. A handy guide to the UK butterflies with information on distribution and biology.

Tolman, T. *Collins Field Guide to the Butterflies of Britain and Europe*, Harper Collins, 1997. This comprehensive book describes 444 species and has over 2,000 colour paintings by the world-renowned butterfly illustrator Richard Lewington.

Waring, P. and Townsend, M. *Field Guide to the Moths of Great Britain and Ireland*, British Wildlife Publications Ltd, 2009 (second edition). A good starting point for those in the UK who want to extend their knowledge and photography to include moths, of which there are many species that can be found in gardens.

Digital photography

Ang, T. *Digital Photographer's Handbook,*, Dorling Kindersley, 2009 (4th edition). All the basics and a lot more, with clearly described information and illustrations.

Plants and gardens

Brickell, C. editor, *The Royal Horticultural Society A to Z Encyclopedia of Garden Plants*, revised 2003 in two volumes, Dorling Kindersley, 2003. Gives information on over 15,500 plants with over 6,000 colour illustrations.

Brickell, C. editor, *The Royal Horticultural Society New Encyclopedia of Plants and Flowers*, Dorling Kindersley, 2006 (4th edition). Gives information on over 8,000 plants with over 4,250 colour illustrations.

Brooklyn Botanic Gardens *Butterfly Gardens: Luring Nature's Loveliest Pollinators to Your Yard*, Brooklyn Botanic Garden Inc, 1995/1996. Information on butterflies and plants for the USA.

Chambers, J. *Wild Flower Gardening*. Ward Lock Ltd, 1989. A good account of wild flower gardening covering all aspects of the plants which are all UK species. There is only brief mention of butterflies and their relationship with the plants.

Creeser, R. *Wildlife Friendly Plants*. Collins and Brown, 2004. Gives photographs and information on a selection of plants suitable for both small and large gardens.

Newman, L.H. and Savonius, M. *Create a Butterfly Garden*, John Baker Ltd, 1967. The original UK butterfly gardening book from the butterfly expert who helped Sir Winston Churchill establish a butterfly garden.

Proctor, M., Yeo, P., Lack, A. *The Natural History of Pollination*, Harper Collins, 1996. An updated edition of the 1973 New Naturalist Series book. Covers all aspects of pollination including a chapter on butterflies and moths.

Rothschild, M. and Farrell, C. *The Butterfly Gardener*, Michael Joseph, 1983. Miriam Rothschild writes eloquently about the outdoor butterfly garden and Clive Farrell introduces the reader to the delights of the indoor tropical butterfly greenhouse. An excellent book by two acknowledged experts.

Proctor, R. *Wild Flowers: Country Classics for the Contemporary Garden*, Cassell Publications, 1991. Although this does not consider butterfly gardening, it covers a wide selection of UK and USA plants with interesting information about them. There are many colour illustrations.

Stevenson, V. *The Wild Garden*, Windward, 1985. A well illustrated account with much practical information. There are planting plans for several gardens and over 300 plants are described with a strong UK bias. Only a few pages are devoted to butterflies and their needs.

Tampion, J. and Tampion, M. *The Living Tropical Greenhouse: Creating a Haven for Butterflies*, Guild of Master Craftsman Publications, 1999.
The how-to book of establishing and maintaining a domestic butterfly greenhouse for breeding and personal study. Although concerned with tropical and sub-tropical species, the principles are applicable to the breeding of temperate species if appropriate changes are made in the plants grown and the internal conditions.

Tekulsky, M. *The Butterfly Garden*. Harvard Common Press, 1985. An interesting book giving introductory information on butterflies and butterfly gardening for the USA with notes on 50 common butterflies and lists of cultivated and wild nectar plants, illustrated with various black and white drawings. Contains an extensive list of further reading.

Verner, Y. *Creating a Flower Meadow*, Green Books Ltd, 1998. A personal account of creating a flower meadow from a disused field with included lists of plants and of butterflies of the UK and USA and a season by season section.

Warren, E.J.M. *The Country Diary Book of Creating a Butterfly Garden*, Webb and Bower with Michael Joseph, 1988. Based around the paintings of Edith Holden, this is a visually attractive book.

DVDs

Because many DVDs are produced by individuals it is worth using the Internet to find out what titles and from where such DVDs are available.

Banks, J. *Diversity in the Rainforest*. A two-part DVD consisting of a 50-minute film of butterflies in the Peruvian rainforest and short clips of some 200 of the species found there. A chance to widen your horizons of the butterfly world without leaving your armchair.

Kemp, R. *Jewels in the Air*, 2006. DVD and pocket field guide. A complete guide, with picture library, to butterfly species breeding in the UK with information on the locations they may be found in.

Roine, A. *The Butterflies of Europe*, 2001. Enquiries to Antti Roine, Tuttulantie 4, FIN-28450 Vanha-Ulvila, Finland. Nearly all the European butterflies and some from adjacent areas are included with photographs, distribution maps and biological information. The user can customize the CD-Rom and add their own data to this flexible and extremely interesting database.

Scott, J.A. *The Butterflies of North America: A Natural History and Field Guide*, 2001, CD-Rom. Hopkins Technology, LCC, 421 Hazel Lane, Hopkins, Minnesota 55343-7116, USA. A truly monumental CD-Rom of the North American species, with thousands of colour paintings, photographs, distribution maps and extensive biological information. A major easy-to-use source and identification aid from this highly respected lepidopterist.

Useful websites

There are thousands of websites that are concerned with butterflies, some specific to a particular country – the following is just a very small selection that you may find useful. There are also websites that have 'butterfly' in the title but have nothing to do with lepidoptera. Readers should note that entomology covers the whole range of insect species and many entomologists also have an interest in other groups of invertebrates. Lepidopterists are interested in everything about butterflies and moths.

www.amentsoc.org
Home site for the UK Amateur Entomologists' Society. One of the UK's leading organizations for people interested in insects. There are adult and junior sections and several journals with articles covering all types of insects from all parts of the world.

www.butterfliesandmoths.org
Comprehensive guide to lepidoptera of the United States and North Mexico.

www.butterfly–conservation.org
Home site for the UK–based Butterfly Conservation, the group with major interest in monitoring and practical conservation of butterflies, moths and their habitats in the UK.

www.butterflyworldproject.com
Home site for the Butterfly World Project at St. Albans, UK. This is a major project for a Visitor Centre in the UK masterminded by Clive Farrell, the country's leading authority on the breeding of tropical butterflies and with practical experience in the establishment of butterfly meadows.

www.flickr.com
The site to find images of anything, including butterflies.

www.lepsoc.org
Home site for the US Lepidopterists' Society. Many activities in the US. Many other countries have an equivalent society.

www.pwbelg.clara.net
The Entomological Livestock Group, based in the UK but open to members from other countries. It issues lists of sales, wants and exchanges of butterfly and moth livestock, and a range of other invertebrates and other relevant materials, including notes on breeding and general information. Usually two information lists are produced each month based on contributions from members.

www.rhs.org.uk
Home site for the Royal Horticultural Society. Lots of information about plants, including plants for butterflies.

www.ukbutterflies.co.uk and www.ukleps.org
Collections of hundreds of images of UK butterflies at all stages of development from egg to adult. Includes information on caterpillar food plants and seasonal periods of adult flights.

www.wwb.co.uk
The website of Worldwide Butterflies, one of the longest–established suppliers of livestock and base of Robert Goodden, the well–known author of many books on butterflies.

About the authors

John and Maureen Tampion have shared a lifelong interest in butterflies and plants. They were educated in Southampton where they met and married. Maureen started a career in law while John pursued an Honours Degree in Botany and a Ph.D. for botanical research studies. They have written extensively on gardening and butterflies, with particular emphasis on temperate and tropical flora and fauna. In 1990 they started their own butterfly and plant photographic library and consultancy.

Over the years John and Maureen have designed and created their many different gardens to maximize visitation by butterflies and other wildlife. They have also grown many unusual plants in their tropical butterfly greenhouses, which have been featured on television, as well as in national newspapers and magazines.

Authors' acknowledgements

All the photographs (except those listed below) are by and copyright of Dr John Tampion. We acknowledge our debt to all other enthusiasts who have spent their lives observing and recording the minute details of butterflies and plants. Without the great benefits of their knowledge and experience we could not have written this book.

Readers may share that knowledge by consulting the books listed under Further Reading (as well as the many other books and articles that we have not had space to include). We also thank everyone at GMC Publications Ltd (especially Virginia Brehaut), all of whom have devoted so much time and effort to producing this revised book.

Photo credits

flickr.com: page 10, audreyjm529; page 26, Muffet; page 31 and 34, steve p2008; page 44, Nieve44/La Luz; page 81, belgianchocolate; page 84, B cool; page 109, ahisgett; page 148, TANAKA Juuyoh; page 156, mikebaird; page 159, Tattooed Hippy; page 163, Rob Young; page 164, me'nthedogs
Wikimedia.org: page 59, Richard Bartz

Index

Illustrations of species are indicated by page numbers in **bold**.

To place an order, or to request a catalogue, contact:
GMC Publications
Castle Place, 166 High Street, Lewes, East Sussex, BN7 1XU
United Kingdom
Tel: +44 (0)1273 488005 Fax: +44 (0)1273 402866
www.gmcbooks.com